NEW YORK CENTRAL

NEW YORK CENTRAL

AARON E. KLEIN

BONANZA BOOKS

NEW YORK

Published 1985 by
Bonanza Books, distributed by
Crown Publishers Inc.

Produced by
Brompton Books Corp.
15 Sherwood Place
Greenwich, CT 06830 USA

Library of Congress Cataloging in Publication Data

Klein, Aaron E.
   New York Central.

   1. New York Central Railroad.   I. Title.
TF25.N6K58   1985   385′.065′74   84-28537
ISBN 05-17-460858

Printed in Hong Kong

ISBN 0-517-46085 8

h g f e

Page 1: Highlands of the
Hudson, *by Leslie Ragan.*
Pages 2-3: *Amtrak's Empire
service runs along the old New
York Central route.*
This page: *The 20th Century
Limited, eastbound.*
Pages 6-7: *E L Henry's
depiction of the first train on
the Mohawk & Hudson in
1831.*

CONTENTS

GEORGE FEATHERSTONAUGH'S GRAND IDEA   6

ERASTUS CORNING'S FIEFDOM   20

THE VANDERBILTS TAKE THE THROTTLE   34

RUNNING A RAILROAD   50

THE TWENTIETH CENTURY   62

DECLINE, MERGER, AND COLLAPSE   86

CHAPTER ONE
GEORGE FEATHERSTONAUGH'S GRAND IDEA

On 23 June 1970 the impossible happened. The Penn Central Transportation Company, the union of the mighty New York Central and Pennsylvania Railroads – then the largest corporate merger ever – entered into reorganization proceedings under the federal bankruptcy law. In years past, the nation's economic structure had been thrown into panic, chaos and depression by far lesser events. But this massive financial disaster caused no 1929-style stock market crash. It did make the front pages of the papers and the network television news; there were the inevitable searching articles in financial and intellectual digests. Wall Street brokers had a lunchtime conversation topic for a while, but for the most part, business in the nation's financial centers went on as usual. Even the Penn Central continued to operate as before. The passenger trains were no later than they had always been, and freight operations were seemingly undisturbed. In a few days the event seemed to fade from the public consciousness.

The collapse of the Penn Central was just one more item in a long, sad series of 'inconceivable' events, starting with the 1963 assassination of John F Kennedy, that seemed to have stunned the American public into a state immune to shock. Hardly a month before, four students had been killed by National Guard troops at Kent State University. The war they were protesting dragged on, as it became more apparent with each day that the United States was losing, militarily and in every other way. To many observers, the merger of the New York Central and the Pennsylvania in 1968 had been more unbelievable than its collapse. But the impact was surely lost in one of the most traumatic years in national history – a year that saw the assassinations of Robert Kennedy and Martin Luther King Jr, and the sordid spectacle of pitched battles in the streets of Chicago at the Democratic National Convention.

If the collapse of the Penn Central had occurred in a more tranquil time, financiers and the general public would have seen it for the truly significant and disastrous event that it was. The Penn-Central's demise was much more than a financial failure. It seemed to portend the collapse of public transportation in the United States, and the inability or unwillingness of the govern-

ment to do anything about it. Eventually the government did do something about it, most significantly in the Acts of Congress that created Amtrak and Conrail. However, at the time of the collapse the future of American railways seemed dark indeed, and there are many who believe that their future is still far from secure.

For those who are familiar with the history of American railroads, particularly that of the New York Central, the collapse of the New York Central/Pennsylvania/Penn Central, not to mention scores of other American railroads, was inevitable. From the very beginning, American rails have been dominated by speculators who saw railroads only as stock certificates to be sold and manipulated for the quickest and greatest profit, rather than as services to provide transport for people and goods. While many of these speculators provided the funds necessary to get railroads started, far too many milked the lines for all they could get, then left the remains to wither away. Excessive government regulation has also contributed to the decline of the American railroad. In many instances, these regulations were needed to protect the public from the speculators and robber barons who owned the railroads. However, the regulations remained in force long after the railroads ceased to be a threat to anyone, severely hampering their struggle for survival in the age of the jet airliner and the superhighway.

The earliest origins of the New York Central stem from a man who was more of a dreamer than a speculator. George Featherstonaugh, a gentleman farmer from a New York town called Duanesburgh, had been fascinated by news of steam railways in England – so much so that he became determined to build one in his home state of New York. If any of Featherstonaugh's neighbors laughed at him, their merriment was not unjustified. In the 1820s, when Featherstonaugh started to formulate his plans, New York was practically the last place in the country, or in the world for that matter, to think about starting a major railroad. The Erie Canal had been opened to traffic in 1825. This great

A prosperous Dutch farm near Batavia served by the line.　　Opposite: *Original Mohawk & Hudson station, Schenectady.*

ditch running from Albany to Buffalo was the largest and most ambitious engineering project that had yet been completed in the young nation. Connecting New York City with the Great Lakes via the Hudson River, the canal promised – and delivered – a new era of prosperity to New York. Many of the most powerful politicians in the state had a financial interest in the canal. They were not about to let anything or anybody emerge as serious competition. In order to build his railroad, Featherstonaugh had to get a charter from the State Legislature, and that seemed to doom the enterprise from the start.

Dreamer though he may have been, Featherstonaugh was realistic enough to know that he would have to present his idea to the legislature in such a way that it was not perceived as a threat to the canal. He also knew that he would need help from someone who had political power. To that end, he traveled some 20 miles to the seat of power in Albany to talk with Stephen Van Rensselaer, the grand old man of the Upstate aristocracy. Van Rensselaer, the last of the old patroons, was probably the richest man in Albany in the 1820s, and he was surely one of the most politically influential. The idea of the railroad intrigued him, and he provided Featherstonaugh with advice, a modest amount of financial support and most importantly, a few well-chosen words to a few well-placed people in the Albany political establishment. Both men knew that the project would have to be modest in scale if it was to have any chance of gaining a charter. A few years before, John Stevens, the American steamboat pioneer, had proposed building a railroad to parallel the Erie Canal, an idea that was swiftly rejected by the canal interests. Featherstonaugh gave notice of his modest proposal in a newspaper called the *Schenectady Cabinet:*

Application will be made to the legislature of the state of New York at the approaching session, for an act to incorporate the Mohawk and Hudson Rail Road Company, with an exclusive grant for a term of years for the construction of a Rail Road betwixt the Mohawk and Hudson Rivers, with a capital investment of three hundred thousand dollars, if necessary; and to receive certain tolls on the same as may seem fit for the legislature to grant. Dated December 19, 1825.

Van Rensselaer and Featherstonaugh had every reason to hope that the proposed 16-mile railroad would be sufficiently nonthreatening to get by the canal interests, which were backed up by a powerful group of politicians, merchants and financiers generally called the Albany Regency. They also knew that the chosen route, between Albany and Schenectady, was located where the Erie Canal was not necessarily the best way to go. The canal ran some forty miles between these points, through a time-consuming series of locks, while the overland distance was only some fifteen miles. Canal boat passengers quickly learned that they could make better time between the two cities by getting off the boat and traveling by horse. While such a change of conveyance may have been convenient for a passenger, it was not particularly expeditious for freight.

As might be expected, the modest proposal encounterd some fierce opposition in the legislature. Many Albanians, as residents of Albany were called, feared that the railroad would bring economic ruin to the city. Van Rensselaer was so pressured by opponents that he told Featherstonaugh he might have to withdraw his support. The railroad was also understandably opposed by the Albany and Schenectady Turnpike Company, a rather badly constructed toll road that was not doing well.

Surprisingly, the charter passed the legislature only a few months after it was introduced and was granted on 17 April 1826. The Mohawk and Hudson, the first of the small lines that were later to merge into the New York Central, while not yet a real enterprise of rails and locomotives, was at least a paper reality. The influence of the canal interests was evident in some of the charter's provisions: the Mohawk and Hudson was to be limited to passenger traffic, and the Erie Canal was to be reimbursed for any losses it might suffer due to the railroad's operations.

Featherstonaugh, still nurturing dreams that his little railroad would some day grow to stretch across the state, now set out to sell stock in the new enterprise. Each share had a par value of $100. As was the custom of the time, the full price did not have to be paid at once. Featherstonaugh hoped to 'call' $30 at the outset, asking for more only if construction costs required it. However, he did not collect as much as he had hoped. Van Rensselaer bought 100 shares, but he paid only $3 on each share — and he had been named president of the company. Many

Albany businessmen began to see the railroad as an advantage for their city, one that would thwart the upstarts in Troy who were beginning to get some of the Erie Canal traffic at Albany's expense. In spite of this change of view on the part of many Albanians, the sale of Mohawk and Hudson stock in Albany began to fall off. At the same time, however, some merchants and speculators in New York City expressed a great deal of interest in the new road. Among these were John Jacob Astor, James Duane and Nicholas Fish. After several meetings with Featherstonaugh and Van Rensselaer, they bought a large block of shares, pumping much-needed capital into the new enterprise. What followed was a scenario that would become all too familiar on American railroads.

While Featherstonaugh's major interest was the railroad itself, the interest of the New York City group was money and money alone. Featherstonaugh, who had been designated vice-

*The Dewitt Clinton entered
service in 1831 between
Albany and Schenectady.*

president, poured all his energy into the Mohawk and Hudson, even taking a trip to England at his own expense to observe the railways there. At the same time, the New York group speculated and manipulated. Featherstonaugh was forced out in 1829. Van Rensselaer's resignation soon followed. One Churchill C Camberling, a close friend of Martin Van Buren (the New York political power who was Vice-President of the United States under Andrew Jackson and became President in 1837) was named president of the Mohawk and Hudson. Once the State powers in New York looked favorably on the little road, the restriction on freight was lifted. The road prospered, and as the New York City group had hoped, the stock soared in value. The speculators sold their stock, reaped their profits and went to look for other financial fields to plow. George Featherstonaugh, the planner and creator who had hoped to be remembered as the builder of a great railroad, disappeared into obscurity.

In 1829 John B Jervis was appointed chief engineer, and the actual building of the line was begun. Most of the 16 miles between Albany and Schenectady constituted a flat plain, presenting no great engineering difficulties. The major problems were the cities themselves, which were built on considerable hills. Steam locomotives of the time were not up to the task of pulling a train of cars up more than the most trifling of inclines. Jervis decided to build inclined planes for moving the cars up and down the Albany and Schenectady hills by means of cables powered by stationary engines. This system remained in operation for some 13 years.

The tracks were of the type called 'strap' rails. These were strips of iron placed on wooden stringers, which rested on stone cubes. The track was laid on a bed of broken stone and earth, and it seemed solid enough, but the stone did not have enough flexibility or 'give' to accommodate the weight of vehicles rolling on the track. What did give from to time were pieces of the strap rail, which snapped loose from the stringers and curved upward in lance-like configurations called 'snakes' or 'snakeheads'; these would sometimes come through the floor of a car, injuring or killing passengers. Strap rail and stone blocks were eventually replaced by 'T-rail' resting on wooden ties.

The track was laid with a footway to accommodate a horse, but the intention was to power the Mohawk and Hudson with steam locomotives. Locomotives had proven their usefulness on English rails, and down in Baltimore Peter Cooper had convinced the directors to go steam with his little demonstration engine, the Tom Thumb. Some of the first locomotives had been imported from England. While the Stourbridge Lion had turned out to be too heavy for the rails of a tiny coal railroad near Honesdale, Pennsylvania, the John Bull was performing well on the Camden and Amboy in New Jersey.

Main picture: *West Point Foundry built the Dewitt Clinton, whose cars resembled stagecoaches of the time.*

Right: *The locomotive Stevens, built in 1850 for the Camden & Amboy Railroad.*

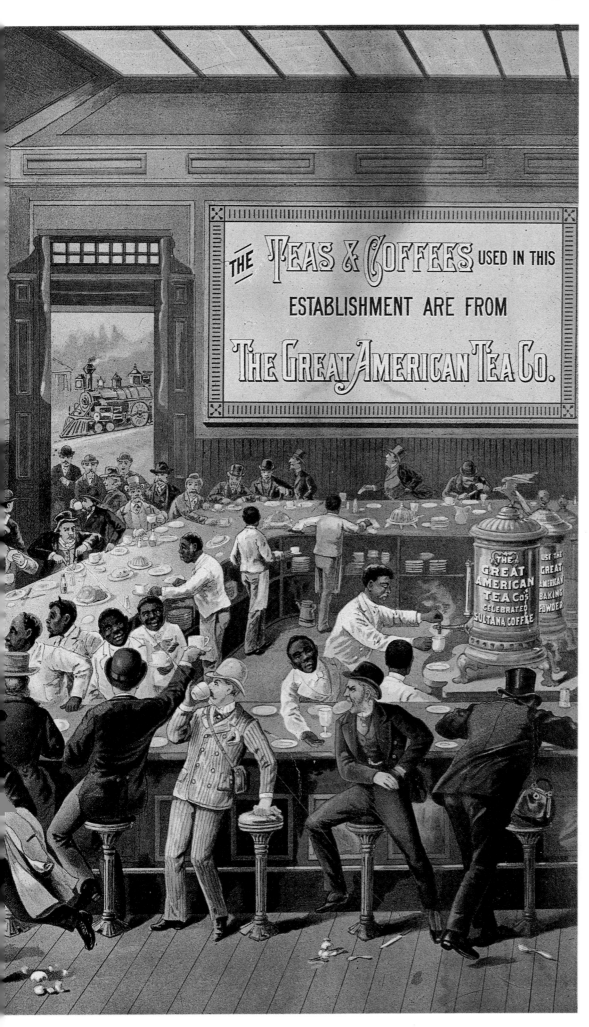

The Great American Tea Company produced this slightly egocentric view of a hasty stop for refreshments.

However, the early American railroads did not have to depend entirely on Britain for their motive power. The West Point Foundry in New York City was building locomotives by the late 1820s. In 1830, this foundry supplied an engine called Best Friend of Charleston for the South Carolina Railroad. This was the locomotive that exploded when the fireman either tied down or sat on the safety valve because the sound of the escaping steam bothered him.

The West Point Foundry built the Mohawk and Hudson's first engine, named the DeWitt Clinton after the eminent New Yorker who was the major driving force behind the Erie Canal. The DeWitt Clinton was a small engine notable for the simplicity of its construction. It weighed some 6758 pounds and was 11.5 feet in length. The engine was mounted on four wheels. Steam was fed to a 5.5-inch diameter cylinder with a 16-inch stroke. While the cylinders of most engines of the time were mounted on the sides of the engine, the DeWitt Clinton's cylinder was mounted at an angle at the rear of the engine. A tender, which was nothing more than a wagon fitted with a canopy, completed the contrivance. Rated at 10 horsepower, the DeWitt Clinton made its first trip at an average speed of 15 mph. However, it was reputed to have reached the breathtaking speed of 30 mph on some of its runs.

The official opening day of the Mohawk and Hudson was 9 August 1831 – a day of celebration. Flags fluttered all over the city of Albany, and excited crowds gathered to look at the DeWitt Clinton spewing smoke and sparks from its tall smokestack. The train consisted of three coaches, which looked (as did most railroad carriages of the time) very much like horse-drawn stage coaches. Passengers sat both inside and atop the coaches. The train started with a jerk so violent that many of the gentlemen's high beaver hats went flying off their heads. It would seem that innovations started immediately. At the first water stop, some fence posts were taken from a farm and wedged between the cars, which greatly reduced the start-up jerk.

People stood along the track to watch the train pass. Some watched from their horse-drawn wagons, and many a frightened horse bolted; there were a number of overturned wagons, collisions and other mishaps, many of which resulted in injuries. When the train arrived in Schenectady it was met by thousands of cheering citizens.

The success of the Mohawk and Hudson soon ended most of the hostility against railroads in New York. Other cities, viewing the material benefits brought to Albany and Schenectady by the railroad, decided they too must have railroads, and so began an intense period of railway construction in New York through the 1830s and 1840s. The rush to build railroads prompted the editor of the Goshen *Independent Republican* to write: 'It is almost impossible to open a paper without finding an account of some railroad meeting. An epidemic on this subject seems to be as prevalent as influenza.'

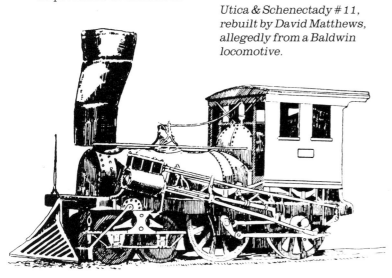

Utica & Schenectady # 11, rebuilt by David Matthews, allegedly from a Baldwin locomotive.

In 1831 notice of a forthcoming 'railroad convention' appeared in a Syracuse newspaper. The convention assembled in Syracuse on 12 October 1831 to discuss a grand enterprise – no less than a railroad all the way across New York from Schenectady to Buffalo. This grandiose scheme never got past the stage of hot air and bluster. Eventually, there would be such a railroad, but it was not to be created in one sweeping move: it would result from the merger of many smaller lines, of which the Mohawk and Hudson was the prototype and inspiration.

It is difficult to determine the chronological order in which the various New York lines were built. Some were incorporated before others, but did not start or complete the lines until others, incorporated at later dates, were finished and in business. The Utica and Schenectady, for example, which connected with the Mohawk and Hudson, was incorporated on 29 August 1833, more than a year after the Tonawanda Railroad Company of Rochester received its charter. However, the Utica and Schenectady was in full operation more than a year before the Tonawanda managed to get a train onto a track.

The Utica and Schenectady ran some 78 miles along the Mohawk Valley between these two cities. Although the New York political and financial establishment was beginning to look more favorably on railroads in the 1830s, the canal interests were still formidable. The legislature was reticent about granting the Utica and Schenectady a charter, since much of the line was to parallel the canal. This juxtaposition encouraged the legislators to lay stiff restrictions on the young Utica and Schenectady. The line was prohibited from carrying any goods other than 'the ordinary baggage of passengers.' It had to pay $22.50 a share for stock in the Mohawk Turnpike, which ran parallel to the proposed railroad. The authorized capital of the Utica and Schenectady was held to $2,000,000, and its corporate existence limited to 50 years. The legislature also decreed that the board of directors must include at least one member from each of the counties through which the line passed. The directors of the new line accepted these restrictions because they had no choice and believed that in time they would be eased or rescinded.

Some relief came from the United States Government in 1837, when a mail-carrying contract was won. In that same year, the legislature granted a small concession when the category of permitted luggage was changed from 'ordinary' to 'any.' However, the railroad was not allowed to charge extra for carrying extra luggage – a ruling that allowed passengers to transport all kinds of goods at no charge through the simple expedient of putting them in a valise. Not until 1844 did the legislature allow the road to carry 'goods and chattels' and then only during seasonal closings of the canal. Even at these times, the Utica and Schenectady had to pay tolls to the state for goods carried.

In spite of these encumbrances, the Utica and Schenectady prospered, partly as a result of the fact that Erastus Corning of Albany was chosen as its first president. Corning was to be the first president of the original New York Central, organized in 1853. (The 'second' New York Central dates from 1914). He served the Utica and Schenectady for 20 years. The only official compensation he received was a silver dinner service. However, as we will see, he more than made up for the lost income when he was president of the New York Central.

The Utica and Schenectady was completed in the summer of 1836. Eight locomotives were ordered from Matthias W Baldwin, who had set up his Philadelphia locomotive factory in 1831. The opening on 1 August 1836 was accompanied by the customary celebration and merriment. The train was met in Utica by practically every citizen of that city, which was often called 'pent-up Utica,' and thousands more. Whatever may have been pent-up seems to have been completely let loose when the two opening-day trains arrived. The city went wild. Drinking, dancing and general carousing continued through the night and into the next day. No one seemed to mind that the trains were several hours late, because the little Baldwin locomotives proved unequal to the task of hauling ten-car trains.

25 CENTS.
FARE FROM
ALBANY TO SCHENECTADY,
BY THE
Mohawk & Hudson
RAILROAD,
2 SHILLINGS.

This Road connects with the Utica and other western roads.

1842.

One of the last Mohawk & Hudson posters, before the name change to Albany & Schenectady.

The Utica and Schenectady did so well that it was able to lay double tracks very soon after opening. After some five years of operation, it could replace the inadequate and dangerous strap rail with iron 'T' rail that was not much different in configuration from the steel rail used today.

The Syracuse and Utica, incorporated on 11 May 1836, ran some 53 miles between these two cities. This road received a better deal from the New York legislature than did the Utica and Schenectady, in that it was permitted to carry freight as well as passengers. However, the line still had to pay tolls to the state during the months the Erie Canal was open. It would be over 30 years before the great waterway yielded precedence to railroads.

The Syracuse and Utica Railroad opened on 3 August 1839 with the usual celebrations. The inordinately long time it took to complete the tracks stemmed from disagreements over whether or not the line was to pass through Rome, New York (it did) and where the tracks were to be laid within the City of Syracuse itself. The city fathers, anxious to have a railroad come to their town, finally agreed to let the tracks run right down Washington Street, the grandest thoroughfare in Syracuse at the time. There they remained until 1937, when the city celebrated their removal. In the interim, Syracuse came to be known as 'that city where the trains run right down the middle of the street.'

The first president of the Syracuse and Utica was John Wilkinson, who had also been postmaster in Syracuse. Wilkinson ran the railroad practically by himself, including the preparation of the annual reports, which he laboriously wrote out by hand. These reports contain much more than earnings and loss figures. Wilkinson included whatever was on his mind, and in so doing provided a fascinating picture of what it was like to run a small railroad in the 1830s and '40s.

The rights of way of early railroads were not fenced off. Consequently, cows and other animals frequently wandered onto the track. Hitting an animal the size of a cow usually resulted in derailment and injury to passengers, a concern that Wilkinson expressed in an annual report:

> There is great hazard in attempting a high rate of speed on account of cattle and other domestic animals which are allowed . . . to run at large; they *will* stray on to the railroad if so allowed. The hazard of injury to passengers from this cause is greater than from any other; and it will increase in proportion to the speed if owners of animals are not required to restrain their going at large.

Passengers who paid no fare were a constant problem of early railroads. Commented Wilkinson in the 1849 annual report:

> The number of persons who pass free upon the railroads in this state is very large and is increasing. This company has endeavored to restrict this number within some reasonable limit, but has not been as successful as desired, by reason of the fact that other companies pass them . . . . We constantly pass great numbers because of inability to pay. That is all proper, but beyond this class of persons it is very questionable whether any should be passed free.

The nonindigent class that Wilkinson referred to were the judges, politicians, prominent merchants and others who thought they were important enough to ride free. Since such people as these had the power to make life miserable for railway

TRAVELLING ON THE MOHAWK AND HUDSON RAIL ROAD:

DEPARTURES FROM STATE-ST. ALBANY.

At   9   o'clock   A. M.
At   11   "   "
At   3   '   P. M.
At   5   "   "
At   9   "   "

DEPARTURES FROM SCHENECTADY.

At   8½   o'clock   P. M.
At   12   "   "
At   3   '   P. M.

And on the arrival of the western stages.

Fare through 50 cents.

N. B. Baggage will be taken to and from the road at Albany by Messrs. Thorp & Sprague's wagons as heretofore at the rate of 6¼ cents for an ordinary travelling trunk, or its equivalent.

Baggage will be taken to and from the Schenectady termination free of expense.

Dec. 30, 1834.   A. WHITNEY, Supt.

Utica, Schenectada, and Albany, *BY RAIL ROAD.*

Trains of Rail-Road Coaches leave as follows:— (Sunday afternoons omitted.)

On and after Sunday, April 1st, two daily lines, leaving Albany at 8½ o'clock A M., and 7½ P M.

On and after April 10th, three daily lines. viz.

From Albany, west,   8½ A. M.   2½ P. M.   7½ night.
Schenectada, west, 9½   "   3½   "   9   "
Utica, east,   9   "   3½   "   9½   "

All baggage must be marked and deposited in the baggage wagon by its owner or person having the charge thereof.

No charge for extra baggage; all baggage positively at the risk of the owner.

Way passengers will attend personally to the disposition of their baggage at Schenectada

WM. C. YOUNG,
(32-ly)   *Superintendent and Engineer.*

managers, catering to them was considered good business.

The Auburn and Syracuse was incorporated on 1 May 1834, some two years before the Syracuse and Utica. Because of financial problems stemming from the Panic of 1837, the 26-mile line was almost abandoned before it was finished. The line was saved by a $200,000 loan from the State of New York, which was approved by the legislature only because of the political power residing in Auburn. This city had been bypassed by the Erie Canal, and the town fathers were understandably miffed at the

New York State's capital was already a bustling rail terminal by the mid-1830s.

prospect of being denied a railroad.

By the summer of 1839, limited horse-powered operations started on the Auburn and Syracuse. The first steam locomotives were running on the line before the summer was over.

The Auburn and Rochester, which was chartered on 13 May 1836, was one of the longest (70 miles) of the railroads that eventually became the New York Central. As was the case with the Auburn and Syracuse, the line was intended to serve cities that had not benefited from the Erie Canal. Since these lines were not in direct competition with the canal, they were not subject to the same operational restrictions imposed by the legislature on lines that paralleled the canal. The Auburn and Rochester, completed in 1841, ran from Auburn through Seneca Falls, Waterloo, Geneva, Manchester and Canandaigua to Rochester.

The Tonawanda Railroad, which received its charter on 24 April 1832, was Rochester's link in the chain of railroads that was being forged across New York. Many citizens of Rochester predicted that their railroad would eventually go all the way to Buffalo, but for the moment Attica, some 42 miles away, was the designated western terminus. The Tonawanda did not get to Attica until 1842, but the road was open and ready for business when tracks between Rochester and Batavia were finished in 1837. The opening of this 34-mile stretch of track was, of course, the excuse for a celebration that was much needed in the hard times following the Panic of 1837. The entry of the first train into Batavia was described in the *Rochester Democrat* of 12 May 1837: 'Passing through one of the most delightful parts of the country the eye ever beheld, we were soon at Batavia. Here was animation. The road for a mile was lined with citizens. The cheers were long and loud, and the thunderings of the cannon, called into requisition on this occasion, responded to the "three times hoorah" which was elicited from the cars by the grand reception.'

The line between Attica and Buffalo, appropriately called the Attica and Buffalo Railroad Company, received its charter in 1836. The road was opened to traffic in 1842. After its completion, a look at a New York railroad map of the period would have suggested that you could now go by rail all the way from the Hudson to Lake Erie without changing cars, assuming that the various railroads would co-operate to provide such a service. Not quite. The Rochester terminus of the Auburn and Rochester was on the west side of the city, while the Tonawanda's station was a few blocks away. The completion of this final connection was delayed for several years, primarily because such businesses as hotels and carriage drivers benefited from the inconvenience caused to passengers by the gap.

While the seven small lines between Albany and Buffalo in 1842 were the nucleus of the first New York Central, there were other lines in the state at the time, some of which would eventually become part of the Central system. In addition, there were several mergers, sales and swaps of lines before and after the formation of the New York Central in 1853.

The Schenectady and Troy Railroad, incorporated in 1836, was probably the first steam railroad in the United States to be owned by a city. The citizens of Troy, New York, had always been envious of the commercial success of Albany. Albany had a greater share of Erie Canal business, even though Troy was closer to the point where the Canal joined the river than its wealthier neighbor six miles downstream. The prospect of a rail link between Albany and Buffalo that would give Albany even greater commercial superiority was more than the 'Trojans' could bear, so they determined to build their own railroad to connect them with the west.

The Schenectady and Troy was originally planned as a private venture with liberal municipal support. However, there was not enough traffic to make the line profitable, so it became a city-owned and -run operation. The Schenectady and Troy was notable for being one of the first, if not the first, of the roads

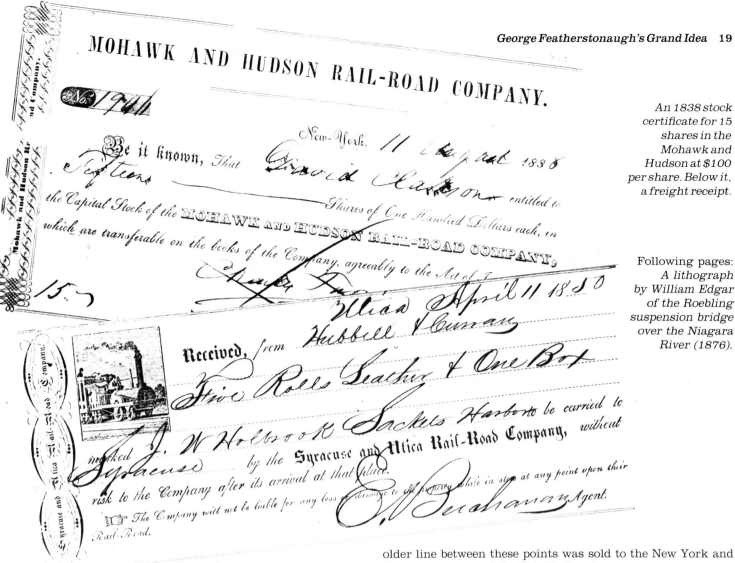

An 1838 stock certificate for 15 shares in the Mohawk and Hudson at $100 per share. Below it, a freight receipt.

Following pages: A lithograph by William Edgar of the Roebling suspension bridge over the Niagara River (1876).

comprising the Central not to use strap rail in its original construction. There is also the well-known story about George Westinghouse, who supposedly got the idea for the air brake after witnessing a minor accident on the Schenectady and Troy.

The Lockport and Niagara Falls Railroad, incorporated in 1834, probably opened for traffic in 1838. Most of the records of this railroad have been lost. The line was later extended to Batavia and Rochester, becoming the Rochester, Lockport and Niagara Falls Railroad in the process. The Buffalo and Lockport Railroad, completed in the early 1850s, provided a more or less direct route between Buffalo and Niagara Falls.

The intention of the Syracuse and Utica Direct Railroad, incorporated in 1852, is implicit in its name. This line covered a considerably shorter distance between these two cities than the previous route, which curved to take in the city of Rome. Some 75 percent of the shares in the new line was owned by stockholders of the old Syracuse and Utica. The other 25 percent was held by stockholders of an ill-fated enterprise called the Syracuse and Utica Straight Line Railroad. Projected along much the same route as the Syracuse and Utica Direct, it was never built. The route was later used by another unsuccessful line, the New York, West Shore and Buffalo. Still later it was the route followed by the Utica-Syracuse high-speed trolley.

Another 'straightening' was accomplished by the 1850 merger of the Auburn and Syracuse and the Auburn and Rochester into a line called the Rochester and Syracuse Railroad Company. The new line replaced a serpentine, single-track line with a direct double-track system between these two important cities. The old line was kept in use for local traffic. The double-track line, which was finished only a month before the formation of the New York Central, became one of its busiest sections.

Another significant merger was that of the Tonawanda and the Attica and Buffalo into the Buffalo and Rochester in 1850. A new direct line was constructed between Batavia and Depew. The older line between these points was sold to the New York and Erie, a precursor of the Erie Railroad.

The Mohawk Valley Railroad, incorporated in 1851, also became part of the New York Central. However, when it was absorbed by the Central, this company existed only as stockholders and a rather distinguished group of directors. No track had been laid, but the route had been surveyed. Two railroads, the little Schenectady and Troy and the Utica and Schenectady, fought furiously for the right to build this line.

The projected route ran mainly along the south side of the Mohawk River, serving towns that had been neglected by the Mohawk and Hudson (now called the Albany and Schenectady). The Schenectady and Troy was annoyed with the Utica and Schenectady because it felt the larger road was not giving it a sufficient share of traffic from the west. In an effort to gain new business and reduce its dependence on the Utica and Schenectady, it petitioned the legislature for a charter to build the line along the south bank of the Mohawk to Utica. The Trojans were nurturing dreams of building a competing line all the way to Buffalo. The people who ran the Utica and Schenectady were not at all keen about any of this, so they filed a protest with the legislature. The contending lines bombarded the legislature with all kinds of lobbying efforts, but the outcome was never in doubt: the Utica and Schenectady had far more political clout than the little line from Troy. The charter was denied.

The group that eventually won a charter to build the Mohawk Valley Railroad was composed mostly of Utica and Schenectady stockholders. Notable among the directors were John V L Pruyn, who was named president of the company, and Erastus Corning. Pruyn provided much of the impetus for forming the New York Central, and, as mentioned before, Erastus Corning became its first president.

The major factor that delayed construction of the Mohawk Valley Railroad was the preoccupation of its executives with a matter of far greater magnitude – the union of the small New York lines into one company.

SUSPENSION BRIDGE

N YORK & BOSTON
TO
CAGO & SAN FRANCISCO

CHAPTER TWO

ERASTUS CORNING'S
FIEFDOM

Although completion of the Attica and Buffalo Railroad in 1843 made it possible to go by rail all the way from Albany to Buffalo, this trip was not one to be undertaken lightly. There were few attempts to co-ordinate the schedules of the various lines, particularly in the salad days of the 1830s and 1840s. Such conveniences as the ability to buy one ticket for the entire trip, and through baggage checking, were slow in coming. However, by the time the final link in the chain was finished, the management of most of the railroads had come to the rather obvious conclusion that co-operation would benefit all of them.

Delegates from all the railroads in the Albany-Buffalo chain met at Albany on 31 January 1843 to discuss ways of co-ordinating their services. Such meetings were the first steps toward the merger that would occur in 1853. The delegates considered such matters as scheduling, how long to allow for food stops and means of running through cars so passengers would not have to change cars at every terminus. The latter was particularly difficult to work out, mainly because of the reluctance of the Schenectady and Troy. This little railroad also ran steamboats down the Hudson to New York City. There was considerable business to be had from city-bound passengers who rode to the Hudson by rail from the west and completed their journey by river steamer. The Schenectady and Troy employed salesmen called 'runners' to ride trains coming into Schenectady and talk passengers into taking their boats from Troy rather than from the Albany docks. The Schenectady and Troy was afraid that through car service would steer too many passengers to Albany, despite the runners' best efforts.

The delegates also adopted a number of resolutions, including one which read in part, 'The several companies upon this Rail Road line will not employ persons in the business of transportation who ever drink intoxicating liquors.' Other resolutions dealt with 'persons who may resort there from curiosity,' that is, loiterers in the station houses, who were sometimes so numerous that passengers had trouble pushing through them to get to the ticket windows. Matters of ticketing and baggage checking were also covered.

By the early 1850s, the unification of the railroads stretching across New York seemed logical if not inevitable. In February of 1851, representatives of ten New York railroads met in Albany to discuss the possiblity of consolidation. In a sense, partial consolidation had already taken place, since some individuals served on the boards of more than one line. At previous meetings

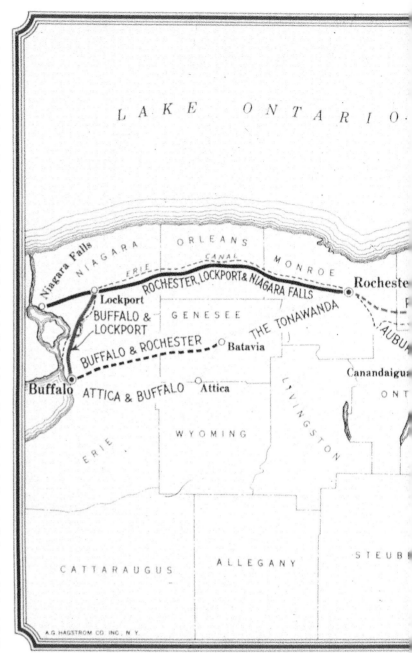

Above: *Ten lines with over 600 miles of track were involved in the consolidation into the New York Central in 1853.*

Left: *An 1852 timetable with the still-familiar disclaimer 'The Company reserve the right to vary . . . at their pleasure.'*

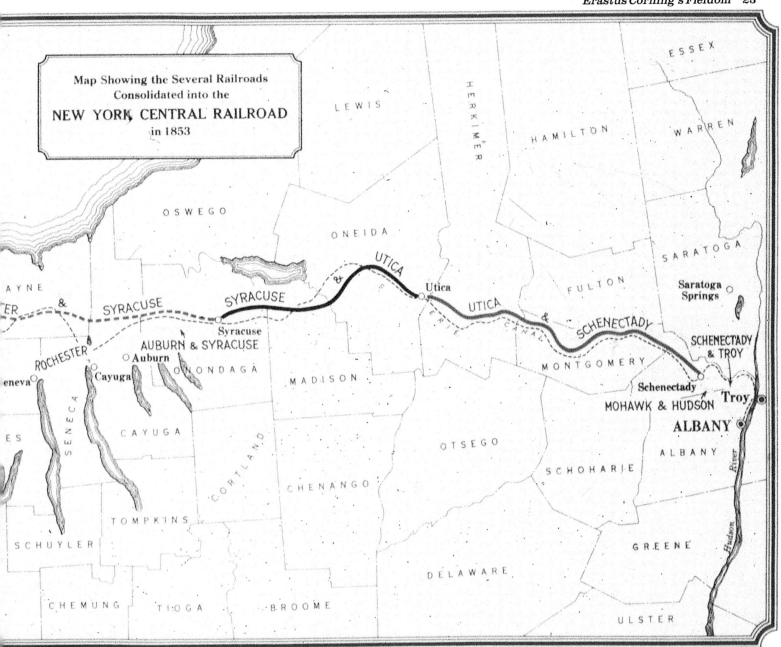

Map Showing the Several Railroads
Consolidated into the
NEW YORK CENTRAL RAILROAD
in 1853

of this kind, resolutions had been adopted urging the legislature to allow mergers of the lines, but the Erie Canal interests had always managed to block passage. At the 1851 meeting, however, the railroaders felt confident that this time they had a good chance of getting their way with the legislature. Railroads had proved to be efficient movers of goods and people, and profitable investment opportunities. Many politically important people, including members of the legislature, now owned stock in railroads The power of the canal group had begun to ebb like water draining from a lock. The measure adopted at the 1851 meeting resolved that: 'A Committee consisting of the Presidents of each Company on the main line between Albany and Buffalo be appointed to make application at the present session of the Legislature for a law authorizing two or more Companies on this Line to consolidate their stock and become one Company.'

The law allowing the merger was passed on 2 April 1853 by a legislature keenly aware of the significance of what it was doing. The various New York lines had the potential to become both the largest railroad and the largest corporation in the nation. New York was a prosperous state that could project huge revenues for railroads. This possibility was not lost on out-of-state lines like the Baltimore and Ohio, which was advancing toward New York, and the Erie, which was already quite active in the state: it had reached Dunkirk and was building across New York toward Lake Erie.

On 5 April 1853 John Pruyn, the secretary of the Utica and Schenectady, sent identical letters to the presidents of the other upstate railroads requesting a meeting to discuss merger plans. A week later, on 12 April, representatives of ten railroads met in Syracuse. The ten lines in attendance, in more or less east-to-west order, were:

Albany and Schenectady
Schenectady and Troy
Utica and Schenectady
Mohawk Valley
Syracuse and Utica
Syracuse and Utica Direct
Rochester and Syracuse
Buffalo and Rochester
Buffalo and Lockport
Rochester, Lockport, and Niagara Falls

The main-line length of these railroads was 298 miles. When the branch lines in existence and under construction were added, the proposed line totaled some 600 plus miles, much of which was double. Although portions of the track, station houses and equipment were in bad repair and some of the more important routes were still single track, it was, for the time, a grand enterprise. The New York Central was capitalized at over $23 million. That seems like a piggy-bank collection by today's standards, but in 1853 it was an enormous amount of money. Indeed, it was almost half the 1853 budget of the United States!

The railroad heads assembled at Albany agreed quickly, in

principle, to a merger. The financial details and decisions on leadership required more intensive negotiation. The basic idea was to swap existing stock for stock in the proposed New York Central. However, the stocks varied in value, and the roads differed widely in their profitability and condition. Some were in great need of repair, while others had been impeccably maintained. Most, no matter how badly they were maintained, or how much money they were losing, wanted premiums above the book value of their stock. Those that were in good physical shape wanted some kind of compensation for the expenditures they had made.

All the lines except the Schenectady and Troy received premiums. These ranged from 17 percent for the Albany and Schenectady that had started it all, to 55 percent for the well-run and profitable Utica and Schenectady and its Mohawk Valley appendage. The hapless Schenectady and Troy was penalized 25 percent. However, its owner, the City of Troy, did not complain too loudly, since its taxpayers were now relieved of the average $100,000-a-year loss that had been sustained by the little railroad.

Presidency of the new railroad went to Erastus Corning, who had done very well with the Utica and Schenectady. In 1853, when he became president of the New York Central, Corning was 59 years old and at the height of his political and financial power. He had long been a formidable presence in the state's Democratic Party organization. He was a close ally of Martin Van Buren, President of the United States from 1837 to 1841, but Van Buren's defeat in the election of 1840 did little, if anything, to diminish Corning's influence. In the 1830s he had been mayor of Albany. Later, he served several terms in the New York State Senate and two terms in Congress as a Representative.

Corning was never defeated in an election. He always stepped down when he felt like it; no one dared to oppose him politically. Corning was far more involved in his varied business interests than he was in holding political office. Among other enterprises,

Below: *The President, one of the first engines built for the New York Central (1855).*

Right: *Chauncey Vibbard, the Central's first superintendent.*

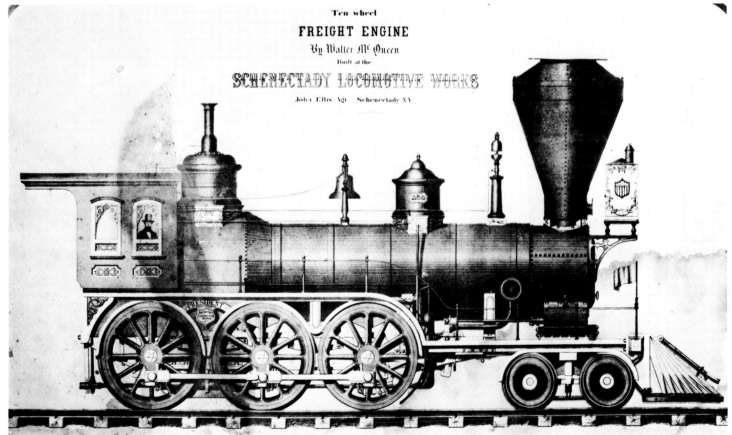

he owned the Albany Iron Works and the Albany Nail Factory. The products of these plants were marketed through a merchandising firm called Corning and Company. He was closely associated with the Albany City Bank, which financed all his enterprises, and he owned large tracts of land in New York and other states, notably Michigan, where he also owned railroad stocks.

Corning's iron factory expanded to produce railroad carriage wheels, and his nail factory started to produce rail spikes at about the time he became president of the Utica and Schenectady. His railroad, and others in New York, became his best customers. The New York Central fit neatly into Corning's plans. It created a self-sustaining personal empire for this Albany merchant prince. Of course, the Central bought its spikes and wheels from Corning. It used his banking services, and served to increase the value of his land holdings. All of this enhanced his political power, enabling him to add to his wealth and influence.

The New York Central Railroad officially came into existence on 6 July 1853. However, the details of the merger had been worked out months before, and there seemed no reason to delay the inevitable celebration. So on Saturday 4 June 1853, there was a weekend excursion from Albany to Niagara Falls and back. This party was an investment in the future. Prominent editors and reporters were invited as well as state legislators and other personages who could be important to the fortunes of the New York Central. Many of the guests were housed at the Delevan House, Albany's newest and most elegant hotel. All other traffic was halted, and the switches were spiked to ensure the fastest possible time. The excursion train averaged 45 miles an hour on the Albany-Niagara Falls trip, which was spectacular for the time and was better than many of today's passenger trains. At Niagara Falls there was a great banquet, followed by many speeches. Among the speakers was William H Seward, who was to be Abraham Lincoln's secretary of state.

The New York Central ran at a loss in 1854, but this was not entirely unexpected. Despite the deficit, Corning insisted on paying a dividend, as he did in other losing years. This was all part of an arrangment with important stockholders. Corning assured them of dividends in return for a free hand in running the railroad: they sent him their proxy ballots signed, but otherwise blank. Corning could then do practically anything he wished, and his mills remained the major suppliers of wheels and spikes to the New York Central. This kind of practice set a precedent that continued into the 1960s, and contributed to the troubles that forced the merger with the Pennsylvania and the collapse of the Penn Central.

With the formation of the New York Central, service on the main line between Albany and New York, and on the branches, improved almost immediately. New cars and locomotives were purchased, and tracks were renovated. The able superintendent of the line, Chauncey Vibbard, had been largely responsible for the efficient operation of the Utica and Schenectady, for which he reportedly drew up the first railroad timetable in the United States. In addition to his responsiblity for New York Central operations and maintenance, Vibbard was charged with getting new business and keeping old customers happy.

Under Vibbard's direction, the ton-miles carried and the revenues generally enjoyed a steady increase. In 1854, about 81,186,000 ton miles were carried. By 1856, ton-miles had increased to 145,733,678. In that year, earnings from freight operations exceeded those from passenger traffic.

Although Vibbard ran an efficient railroad, the Central was not without safety problems. Wrecks were far too common on all American railroads in the nineteenth century. These accidents were the inevitable results of primitive or nonexistent signaling, mechanical defects in tracks and equipment and carelessness. Broken axles and tracks, and collapsed bridges, were frequent ingredients of these wrecks.

The Niagara Falls Bridge increased the popularity of excursions to a much-frequented attraction.

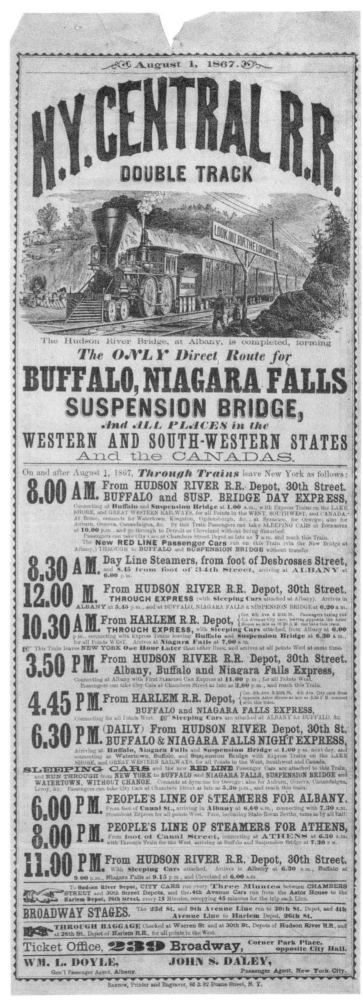

In an 1856 wreck, an axle on an express train from Albany broke, causing cars to tumble down an embankment. One of Vibbard's nephews was killed in this accident. In that same year, a night express crashed into the rear of a cattle train, killing six workmen who were sleeping in the rear car. In 1858 a train derailed and piled up on a bridge over Sauquoit Creek, west of Utica. Another train plowed into the wreckage. Eight died and scores were injured. Animals on the tracks continued to be a problem. In one freakish 1855 accident, the locomotive, tender, baggage car and two passenger cars ran over a horse without derailment or other incident. But the third passenger car derailed, killing one passenger and injuring several others.

The cause of the wreck on the Sauquoit Creek Bridge was found to be the bridge itself, which led to an investigation of all bridges on the system. Of particular concern was the great suspension bridge over the Niagara River about a mile below the falls. This bridge, one of the wonders of the age, was designed by John A Roebling, who is better known as the designer of the Brooklyn Bridge. John Roebling died of tetanus in 1869, after his foot was crushed by a ferry boat as he was surveying a tower site for the Brooklyn Bridge. The bridge was finished by his son, Washington Roebling, who suffered terribly from the bends, an affliction he obtained from working in deeply immersed caissons. To start the Niagara River Bridge, Roebling flew a kite over the Niagara River. An associate on the Canadian side of the river hauled down the cord, which was used to bring over a heavier cord, and so on in turn until transmittal of the wires that were spun into the suspension cables.

Quite a few observers predicted that the bridge would collapse the first time a train went over it. The first train, a 22-car,

An American-type 4-4-0
engine of 1872, three years
after the merger of the Central
and the Hudson River
Railroad under the aegis of
'Commodore' Vanderbilt.

Left: *A Nast caricature of
'Boss' Tweed, who ran the
notorious Tammany Ring.*

Opposite: *The Lake Shore
Railroad, bordering Lake Erie,
gave access to the Middle West.*

into the Central's purchasing practices, but also into the way the stock swaps had been done. Apparently, some shady dealings in New York and Harlem stock down in New York City had caused some New York Central stockholders to start wondering if the shifty ways of the city crowd might have rubbed off on the Central leadership.

A very angry John Pruyn responded to the allegations by calling on the board of directors to conduct an investigation. A committe made up of two stockholders and a member of the board carried out the investigation of the financial transactions involved with the merger. It was one of the most meticulous inquiries ever carried out. In those days of no computers or adding machines, all the ledger-book entries and mathematical calculations were laboriously made with pen and ink, and these figures were gone over by the investigators in the same painstaking way. When all this paperwork was finished, the committee reported that a comparison between the records of the railroad and those of the banks with which it had dealings revealed a discrepancy of 20 cents. This turned out to be a bank error.

While the committee found there were no problems in connection with stock transfers, they did make some recommendations to safeguard against the possibility of stock frauds in the future. They proposed registration of stock transfers with independent agencies. Such practices are standard procedure today, but in the 1850s, they were considered radical and dangerous by many financiers. The Board of Brokers of the New York Stock Exchange was not at all receptive to the plan. When the New York Central insisted on going ahead with registration, it was barred from the Exchange. The Central persisted in its plans, and the New York Stock Exchange readmitted the company in December of 1855.

The investigation of the Central's purchasing practices also resulted in a general vindication, but Corning did not escape a few mild rebukes. The investigating committee came to the conclusion that Corning had not cheated the railroad in any way. On the matter of the spikes, wheels and rails the committee stated: 'These prices are not, in general, placed above the market rates of the same kind of articles elsewhere, but in relation to the iron rails purchased, this Committee do not think that the New York Central Railroad Company, or any other large Railroad Company, should pay a commission to any one on this side of the Atlantic for importing railroad iron.'

The Committee also suggested that 'The principle of buying articles required for the use of the Railroad Company from its own officers might in time come to lead to abuses of great magnitude. The Committee are of the opinion that the system of purchases . . . should be placed under such regulations and restrictions by the Directors as they may deem best calculated to protect the interests of the Company.'

Corning was more than a little hurt and angry. Nevertheless, he announced that firms other than his own would have a chance at dealing with the Central, and that he was forthwith returning the sum of $10,000 – which he claimed represented the total profits gained by Corning and Company in its transactions with the Central.

Corning's resentment was understandable in the context of his times, when even large companies were often closely identified with one person, who ruled like a family patriarch and condoned no opposition. Corning and everyone else knew that many other corporate heads engaged in the same sort of practices the investigating committee had criticized. He may well have regarded his detractors as ungrateful children who were violating the commandment to honor one's father.

Ultimately, the reprimands and criticisms from newspapers and committees did little to deter Corning from pursuing policies he saw as advantageous to the Central and its stockholders. He believed it was important to extend the Central's operations

350-ton freight train, crossed the bridge on 17 March 1855: at one point, the entire train was on the bridge. The span hardly shook as the train rumbled over in a blinding snow squall. The inspectors found the bridge to be sound, and for many years it provided important access to Upper Canada, Detroit, Chicago and the West. A junction village called Suspension Bridge grew up around the span.

Bridges and tracks were not the only objects of investigation on the New York Central. Corning's financial practices also came under scrutiny. His total profits in the exchange of stocks and bonds accompanying the merger were around $100,000, a formidable sum in the 1850s. Almost before the ink was dry on the merger agreements, Corning announced a much-needed major improvement and renovation program. The bank that provided the funds was the Albany City Bank. With this money, new rails were imported from England by Corning and Company, which received a 2.5 percent commission on the transaction. The railroad spent $84,000 on spikes and $71,000 on new wheels – all of them purchased from Corning's factories. The rails would probably have been purchased from Corning too, if his foundry had been equipped to make them. When he decreed that the Central needed more land, it was bought – from Corning companies.

Corning saw nothing wrong in any of this. He maintained that his prices were fair, and that he even threw a little business to other companies from time to time. However, some New York newspapers did not take the matter so lightly. Nor did some groups of stockholders, who began to call for inquiries, not only

westward toward fast-growing cities like Cincinnati, Detroit and Chicago. Actually, Corning's interest in the West had started before the merger. In 1851 he had pushed through a bill in the New York Legislature allowing railroads in the state to purchase stock in the Great Western of Canada. Corning bought quite a bit of that stock, and served on the Great Western board of directors until he was named president of the New York Central. When the Central was formed, the various lines gave up their stock to the New York Central Company. Corning, however, held on to his own shares, and it hardly seems necessary to name the companies from which the Great Western bought its spikes and wheels. Some Canadian companies complained about the

Great Western buying from Corning but these complaints caused him little inconvenience.

The Great Western ran from the western bank of the Niagara River opposite Buffalo through the southern peninsula of Ontario to Detroit. With completion of the bridge across the Niagara River, the new western cities were open to New York rails.

Two other lines attracted Corning's interest: the Buffalo and State Line Railroad and the Michigan Central Railroad. The Buffalo and State Line, later renamed the Lake Shore, ran for about 68 miles along the south shore of Lake Erie to the Pennsylvania border. The enterprise was a joint venture between the

The Putnam, a 4-4-0 locomotive of the post-Civil War era.

Erie Railroad and a group from the New York lines. Daniel Drew, who was later to fight many a battle with the New York Central, was on the board, and Dean Richmond, the first vice-president of the New York Central, was the president. It was a stormy relationship, in which the two men disagreed frequently. The most serious battle, occurring at the start of the enterprise, was over gauge. The Erie employed broad gauge, while the New York lines used standard gauge. Richmond, with Corning's help, got the Buffalo and State Line to adopt standard gauge, opening the new line to rolling stock from the New York lines, and closing it, at least for the moment, to the Erie. At the time of the Central merger, the various New York lines owned about $400,000 in Buffalo and State Line stock, all of which was turned over to the New York Central.

Corning bought his first stock in the Michigan Central in 1846, thereby gaining, of course, another customer for spikes, wheels and rails. At the same time, he started to buy large parcels of land in areas projected to be served by the Michigan Central. The Michigan Central then bought into a number of small Illinois lines, which later merged to form the Chicago, Burlington, and Quincy. This move had the potential of opening up Chicago for Corning, who did not have complete control of lines to Chicago and other cities to the west. The New York Central did not extend its lines outright to Chicago until the

New York City was the focal point of an 1850s rate war between the Central and the Erie; ironically, neither had direct access to the city at the time.

Vanderbilt era. However, the crafty old Albany merchant did have enough say in the running of the lines between Buffalo, Detroit and Chicago to make the time and thought he spent on them very much worth his while.

During Corning's tenure, there was no direct rail link between the New York Central and New York City, and he seemed to want things that way. The Hudson River provided a dependable, maintenance-free way to get to New York City from Albany, and the shipping interests in that city were happy enough with the situation as it existed, even though the river was often frozen several months of the year. Corning did make some efforts to gain access to Boston through an arrangment with the Boston and Worcester Railroad. That venture was not notably successful. Very little traffic was sent to Troy, even though there was a railroad bridge across the Hudson at that city. It would seem that Corning was determined to make Albany the premier city of the state, and to keep Troy in a subordinate position. Eventually, Russell Sage, Troy's representative on the New York Central board, was eased out.

The New York Central faced some stiff competition for traffic from the eastern seaboard to the inland cities. Apart from the Erie Canal, the Baltimore and Ohio, the Pennsylvania and the Erie Railroads were rapidly expanding their operations westward in the 1850s. Canada's Grand Trunk was also getting a healthy share of the traffic. The rate structures were inconsistent and confusing. Various local issues dictated what rates a railroad could charge. For example, if the New York Central lowered its rates in New York to compete with the Erie Railroad, it might be accused of trying to destroy the Erie Canal, which still had a large body of supporters.

Corning's philosophy was that you tried to make money by beating out your competitors, but if you started to lose money in these efforts, the next thing to try was co-operation. With that in mind, he called a meeting of the railroads engaged in traffic from the northeastern seaboard to the interior, for the purpose of discussing ways to co-operate. The meeting was held at the St Nicholas Hotel in New York City in 1854. In addition to representatives from the Pennsylvania, the Baltimore and Ohio, the Erie (then called the New York and Erie), and the Boston and Albany, several smaller lines, including the Corning vassal lines (Michigan Central, Buffalo and State Line), were in attendance.

Corning proposed uniform rates, and an end to some of the cutthroat tactics used by the lines to steal business from one another. Among the latter were runners who lured travelers with exaggerated claims of the merits of their own line and horror tales about the competition. Corning wanted each railroad to respect the territory of the others, and in general to establish what he saw as a community of interests.

The railroads in attendance accepted what came to be called the 'St Nicholas Agreement,' but not for long. The agreement was immediately attacked as a conspiracy to swindle the public. The *Syracuse Chronicle* called it 'swindling and roguery,' in a story that went on to say: 'The combination embraces a giant scheme for plunder . . . It has been tried often before, but has never had a permanent success in this country. A monopoly here cannot stand against the general dissatisfaction of the public. It breeds mobs; violence to railroad property; a tearing up of the tracks, a burning of the car houses, etc., etc., and has uniformly proved disastrous to those who have shouldered it.' The *New York Times* blasted the agreement as 'a combination of the railroad companies against the public.'

The agreement, which went into effect on 1 September 1854, lasted barely six months. Its demise was not due to public outrage, but to the inability of the roads to abide by its provisions. By March of 1855, the Erie had withdrawn, and the first of a series of rate wars and other battles between the Erie and New York Central began.

The Erie reduced its passenger fares to New York City, and the Central opened a ticket office there. Both lines were somewhat presumptuous in boasting of service to New York City, since neither road had tracks into the city. The Central completed the journey by Hudson River steamer, and the Erie's tracks ended on the west bank of the Hudson at a village called Piermont.

The Erie shot first by reducing its New York-Buffalo fare to $2.50 under that of the Central. Corning responded by starting a 'cheap train' with fares $1.25 or $2.50 less than the Erie's, depending on whether the trip was all rail, or part rail and part water. At that time, a Central passenger had the choice of making the New York-Albany leg of the trip by river steamer or on the rails of the New York and Harlem Railroad and Hudson River Railroad to Chatham Four Corners, where connection was made with the Boston and Albany to complete the trip to Albany. Before the Central had its own tracks into New York, the Hudson River route was far more popular. It was convenient, scenic and $1.25 cheaper than the all-rail route.

The adversaries began to lose money and agreed to a truce, which lasted only a few months. By the spring of 1857 they were at it again, clashing over trains from Chicago. At this time, the Lake Shore Railroad was being assembled from the Buffalo and State Line and a few other lines. This new railroad started a fast service from Chicago to Buffalo and Dunkirk, New York, from which points both the Erie and the Central could provide connections to New York City. When the Erie cut its fares sharply, the Central used its considerable influence with the Buffalo and State Line to persuade that road to refuse to honor Erie tickets. Any passsenger holding an Erie ticket who wished to continue on the Central was charged a double fare. Daniel Drew, the treaurer of the Erie, and a big stockholder in the Buffalo and State Line, was furious; he retaliated by sharply reducing fares on the Erie's Buffalo-New York trains.

The two rivals then began a battle – literally – of broadsides. They published large posters, or broadsides, that appeared in newspapers and were pasted on the sides of buildings to warn passengers of the awful things they might have to endure if they took the 'other' railroad to New York. In these posters, the New York Central claimed to be the only railroad that 'can land passengers by Cars in New York City within a short distance of the principal hotels.' This was true, in a sense, but the posters failed to mention that the trip involved a ferry ride across the Hudson to make connections with the Hudson River Railroad. You can be sure the Erie's posters made up for the Central's omissions. One Erie poster featured a lengthy letter that had been written to the *New York Herald* by some apparently disgruntled New York Central passengers. Among other things, the complainants wrote, 'Instead of coming directly to New York, we were landed at Albany, where after a detention of about an hour, we were ferried across the Hudson River and, by dint of walking fifteen or twenty rods through the mud, reached the cars of the Hudson River Railroad.' They went on to say that because the Erie Railroad trains got to New York so much earlier than they did, all the hotels were filled up.

There were a few more attempts to establish peace, but the Erie continued to slash its Buffalo-New York fares. A number of railroad conventions were held in the summer of 1858, at which the assembled railroad representatives discussed what to do about the misbehaving Erie. At one of these meetings, a resolution was passed not to honor Erie interchange tickets until the Erie came around. However, not all the railroads agreed to this action.

The Erie's aggressive rate-slashing did little to slow its steady decline, or to seriously hamper the Central's generally strong position in New York. However, it was becoming clear that no New York State railroad could maintain a dominant position for long unless it had direct access to New York City. The Central did not gain such access until after the Civil War. The impetus and drive for this accomplishment did not come from Erastus Corning and his Albany cabal of merchant capitalists, but from a new breed: the postwar industrial capitalist. This group included men like John D Rockefeller, Andrew Carnegie and Cornelius Vanderbilt. By the time they had swept across the country with the energy of a force of nature, the likes of Erastus Corning had gone the way of the dinosaur.

CHAPTER THREE

THE VANDERBILTS TAKE THE THROTTLE

The history of the modern New York Central Railroad and the Vanderbilt family saga are practically the same story. Yet in the 1830s, when the rail links that would become the New York Central were being forged, Cornelius Vanderbilt, founder and patriarch of the Vanderbilt clan, had no interest at all in railroads. Prophetically enough, however, he was already in conflict with Daniel Drew, the man who for years was to be his chief railroad adversary.

Cornelius Vanderbilt, born in Port Richmond on Staten Island in 1794, is the personification of the American poor-boy-makes-good success story. His paternal ancestors, Dutch settlers who came to Long Island in the late seventeenth century, spelled the family name van der Bilt. His father was a farmer who earned a little extra money from time to time transporting goods and people around New York Harbor in a small boat.

Young Cornelius learned to sail and to lighter – that is, take cargo from larger vessels at anchor and sail it to shore – by helping his father. By the age of 16, he had started his first business. With $100 borrowed from his parents, he bought a periauger, a small sailboat common in the waters between Manhattan and Staten Island at the time. With this boat he ran a ferry service between these two islands. When he was 19, he married his cousin, Sophia Johnson. During the War of 1812 he had a contract with the government to provision the forts in and around New York Harbor. He made quite a bit of money – enough to buy and build several vessels. These he operated as traders and cargo vessels along the eastern seaboard from New England as far south as Charleston.

In 1818 he sold his vessels and went to work as a captain for one Thomas Gibbons, who ran a ferry service beween New Brunswick, New Jersey, and New York City via the Raritan River. This move surprised people who knew Vanderbilt. For one thing, he had never worked for anyone but himself; besides that, Gibbons ran steamboats, for which Vanderbilt had expressed nothing but contempt until this time. It is believed that whatever his personal opinion of steamboats, he knew where the future of shipping lay, and working for Gibbons was a chance to learn his way around steamboats without making a large investment.

At the time Vanderbilt went to work for Gibbons, Robert Fulton had a monopoly on steam navigation in New York Harbor.

The monopoly was violated by almost everyone and Gibbons was no exception. He had brought suit against Fulton, but their battles were not limited to the courtroom. Gibbons regularly sent his boats into New York waters, and the resulting confrontations were often violent. Vanderbilt proved to be particularly adept at avoiding the deputy sheriffs sent out to arrest anyone entering New York waters in violation of the monopoly. Gibbons won the suit, and the monopoly was ruled unconstitutional by the Supreme Court in 1824.

Vanderbilt was in the employ of Gibbons for 11 years. During that time he was instrumental in transforming Gibbons' operation from a perennial money-loser to one of the most successful shipping companies on the eastern seaboard. The line expanded from one small steamer to a multi-vessel fleet. During this time Vanderbilt engaged in a few enterprises of his own. He bought a rundown tavern on the banks of the Raritan River and turned it into a hotel called Bellona Hall after the *Bellona*, a large steamer he had persuaded Gibbons to build. Mrs Vanderbilt was put in charge of this hostelry, which prospered as one of the better-known refreshment centers for New York-Philadelphia travelers. While turning Bellona Hall into a fine hotel, renowned for its food and service, Mrs Vanderbilt somehow found time to deliver a baby about every two years; she had thirteen children.

In the late 1820s, Vanderbilt decided he had accumulated enough capital and knowledge to start his own shipping enterprise. He sold Bellona Hall and moved his family to New York City. Mrs Vanderbilt was bitterly opposed to this move, but it would seem that Vanderbilt always got his way. He started operations on the Hudson, between New York City and Peekskill, in the 1830s and was soon engaged in his first battles with Daniel Drew, who was also operating Hudson River steamers betwen these points at the time. Vanderbilt immediately engaged Drew in a rate war. In 1834, when the fare between New York City and Peekskill was down to 12.5 cents (one 'bit'), Drew sold out.

After eliminating Drew, Vanderbilt extended his operations to Albany, taking on the powerful Hudson River Association in a rate war. With only two boats, he soon had his larger competitors begging. They agreed to pay him a huge sum to stay out of their waters for ten years' time.

Vanderbilt then turned his attention to Long Island Sound, establishing steamer service to Providence and Boston. By the mid-1840s he was a millionaire, and anxious to gain a place for himself and his family in New York society. But this coarse, tobacco-chewing, profane oaf of a man was emphatically rebuffed by the Manahattan socialites. Always eager for a fight, Vanderbilt soon made himself a personage so important that no one dared to cross him. Eventually, his family name came to be practically synonymous with all that was high in society. His wife, less eager to throw herself into the Manhattan social arena, would have been content to live out her days in the lavish Staten Island mansion Vanderbilt had constructed in 1840. But the shipping tycoon was determined to show those fancy Manhattanites that he was not to be denied, and he started to build a town house on Washington Place. In typical fashion, he bulled ahead with his plans, brushing aside Mrs Vanderbilt's tearful protests. She finally had a nervous breakdown and was admitted to a sanitorium, where she remained for only a few months before dutifully moving into the New York townhouse.

The California gold rush of 1849 was very profitable for Vanderbilt, who was too smart to be a prospector. Many Forty-niners made the trip to California via the Isthmus of Panama. This route involved a dangerous muleback trek through the thick Panamanian rain forest. Vanderbilt offered a route through Nicaragua, which was a little longer than the Panama route, but considerably safer and usually faster. He established a company called the American Atlantic and Pacific Ship Canal Co. The

Previous pages: *The powerful Erie Railroad eluded the Vanderbilts' grasp.*

Left: *Cornelius Vanderbilt.*

Acquisition of the
New York and Harlem
was a coup for the
Central.

name of the company reveals the grand scheme Vanderbilt had in mind: in fact, he wanted to build a canal across Nicaragua, but he failed to raise the needed capital. This was one of the few times in his life that the Commodore, as he was now widely called, did not get what he wanted. Nevertheless, he dredged parts of the San Juan River, built docks on both the Pacific and Atlantic coasts of Nicaragua, and constructed a 12-mile paved road from Lake Nicaragua to the Pacific Coast. Thus Vanderbilt could provide passage across Nicaragua in the relative comfort of lake and river steamer and stagecoach at a lower fare than that charged by his competitors, who subjected their customers to the dangerous mule ride through the jungle.

The Nicaragua operation, called the Accessory Transit Company, made so much money that Vanderbilt decided to treat himself, his family and a few selected friends to a vacation — Vanderbilt style. He built a steam yacht, the *North Star*, expressly for this purpose and in 1853 embarked on a grand tour of Europe with his entourage.

Vanderbilt left the management of the Accessory Transit Company to a pair of subordinates, who manipulated the stock and essentially stole the company. At about the same time, the American soldier of fortune and adventurer William Walker had seized control of Nicaragua. He rescinded Vanderbilt's charter to run the Accessory Transit Company, turning it over to the two stock manipulators.

Vanderbilt's approach to this situation was, again, typical of the direct, effective and ruthless way he eliminated problems. To the stock manipulators he sent a short note: 'You have undertaken to cheat me. I won't sue you, for the law is too slow. I'll ruin you.' He did just that. In a matter of weeks, he outmaneuvered his rivals and had his company back. He then determined to have Walker thrown out of Nicaragua, and that bit of business was accomplished by 1857.

As soon as he got his Nicaragua operation back, Vanderbilt told his frightened competitors that he would not reopen the business if they would pay him $40,000 a month. They agreed to this, and when Vanderbilt raised the fee to $56,000 a month, they had no choice but to pay the additional sum.

Vanderbilt did not express any overt interest in railroads until he was almost 70, when he started to buy stock in the New York

The Vanderbilt name was synonymous with American railroading by the 1880s.

and Harlem Railroad (1862). This little line had originally been chartered in 1831 to operate from 23rd Street, then the northern edge of New York City, to the little village of Harlem on the northern tip of Manhattan Island. Twenty-third Street turned out to be too far north, and the charter was revised to allow operations from Prince Street. By 1852 the line had been extended 131 miles north to Chatham Four Corners. There passengers could make connections for Albany, although actual access to the city was only by Hudson River ferry.

Vanderbilt was also interested in the Hudson River Railroad and by 1863 had obtained a few shares in this line, which ran along the east bank of the river. It was organized by a group of Poughkeepsie businessmen in 1842, largely in response to the need for transportation during the winter months when the Hudson was frozen over. Construction problems were formidable, and the first section between New York and Peekskill was not opened until 1849. Service to Albany, via Hudson River ferry, was available by 1851. The line did not prosper, and by the time Vanderbilt started to buy shares, it was in disrepair and near bankruptcy.

Once Vanderbilt had taken an interest in railroads, he went after what he wanted with his customary zeal and ruthlessness. He bought New York and Harlem stock at $9.00 a share; through skillful manipulation, the price soared to $50. At this point he bribed members of the New York Common Council, then under the control of William Marcy ('Boss') Tweed, to extend the New York and Harlem southward as a street car line from 42nd Street to the Battery. The stock shot up again to more than ten times its original value.

Daniel Drew was not at all happy with Vanderbilt's coup. He too plotted with the council and found that it was just as willing to take his bribes as Vanderbilt's. The idea was to get the council to rescind the extension charter, then buy up the stock as its price dropped in response. But Vanderbilt knew what was happening. He hed set aside a large fund for buying up every share of New York and Harlem, thereby keeping the price up. It also seemed that the Drew gang was selling more shares than actually existed. The plotters, including several members of the New York Common Council, had to make good on the shares, which were now valued at $179. Vanderbilt made millions and took

control of the New York and Harlem, which he left in the charge of his son, William.

Next on Vanderbilt's agenda was a merger of the New York and Harlem with the Hudson River Railroad. For this he needed permission from the New York State Legislature. Accordingly, he traveled to Albany to persuade the public servants with verbal and other, more tangible, inducements. The word got around Wall Street, and Hudson River Railroad stock moved up from $25 toward $150. Drew, however, looking for revenge, had been busy 'persuading' quite a few legislators not to approve the merger, again hoping to drive the stock down and sell it 'short.' For a while, it was not clear who would be able to buy the most legislators. Vanderbilt again bought up the stock as it was offered, directing the battle from his Washington Place mansion. The result was almost an exact repeat of Drew's previous attempt to best Vanderbilt: Drew's forces sold more stock than existed, and had to make an expensive settlement.

The Commodore was now ready to take in the New York Central. However, Erastus Corning and the Albany Old Guard were not about to hand over the Central to that boorish lout from Staten Island without a fight. Vanderbilt had held a few shares of Central stock since 1863, and had made it quite clear that he would like a seat on the board; Corning had made it equally clear that he did not want the Commodore in any situation that would make it easier for him to assume control. Although they were business rivals, there was no animosity between them. Repre-

Above: The New York Central Station at 138th Street, New York City.

Opposite: Downtown New York, site of the Hudson River Railroad freight yards.

sentatives from the Hudson and the New York Central had met in 1866 to discuss ways of increasing co-operation between the lines. The boards were unable to reach an agreement, but the two principals reportedly agreed that it would have been possible had no third party been involved. Once it was clear, however, that the Central was not going to co-operate with him, Vanderbilt went after the line in his own style.

By the 1860s some members of the Central board had become impatient with Corning's leadership. He was regarded as being too cautious and out of step with the changing times. Corning continued to ship goods by river steamer from Albany to New York, even though he could have shipped by rail all the way to New York if he had agreed to construction of a bridge over the Hudson to connect with the Hudson River Railroad. Corning made use of the Hudson River Railroad only when the river was frozen.

Thomas Olcutt, a member of the board from Albany, had attempted to remove Corning on several occasions, enlisting the aid of Dean Richmond of Buffalo. Richmond wanted the Central to use rails all the way from Buffalo to New York, even though he owned Lake Erie steamers. He felt that he should be the next president of the Central, but believed that Corning planned to name Pruyn as his successor — a circumstance that contributed to Richmond's eagerness to oust Corning.

Olcutt launched another campaign against Corning in 1864, and this time it appeared that he had Vanderbilt's support. Corning did not feel up to a fight, and he let Vanderbilt know that he was willing to compromise. The two old campaigners met and worked out their deal. Corning would resign from the presidency, but retain a seat on the board. Richmond would become the new president and get the Central board to agree to the trans-Hudson bridge connecting the Central with the Hudson River Railroad. Richmond bought Hudson shares and assumed a seat on the board. A merger between the New York Central and the Hudson River Railroad now seemed inevitable.

The bridge was built, and all appeared to be going as planned, when Daniel Drew, still aching for revenge, tried again to upset Vanderbilt's plans. Drew owned a Hudson River steamboat line, and he feared a serious loss of business if the Central and the Hudson joined. The usual tactic of bribing legislators could not stop the movement toward merger. The best he could hope to do was delay action long enough to devise an alternative. Richmond's forces worked out a merger agreement, and things seemed to be going Vanderbilt's way, when Richmond died.

Upon Richmond's death, a new force entered the field of combat. William Fargo, one of the founders of the Wells Fargo

Main picture: *The imposing new Grand Central Depot at 42nd Street and Fourth Avenue.*

Above: *An interior view of the terminal from* Leslie's Illustrated Newspaper.

Company, had bought enough Central stock to become a power in the organization. In collaboration with two Wall Street brokers, LeGrand Lockwood and Henry ('the Silent') Keep, he planned to manipulate the stock to mutual advantage and leave the Central to rot. Much the same had happened to the Erie under Drew, to the point where it became known as 'two streaks of rust.' Henry the Silent was anxious to get back at Vanderbilt, because the Commodore had once soured one of Keep's deals, resulting in losses of hundreds of thousands. The plan was to sell the stock short, announce that the merger deal was off and then reap profits as the stock went down.

Vanderbilt was again on top of the situation; he sold 60,000 shares before the price went down, with righteous statements that he wanted nothing to do with a company 'owned by such men' as Keep and Fargo. What happened next made it seem that Vanderbilt was in command of the forces of nature. The winter turned unusually bitter, and the Hudson froze with a solidity that could not be denied. As had always been the case, the New York Central planned to transfer its shipments to the Hudson River Railroad. On 15 January Vanderbilt struck his mighty blow. He announced that the Hudson River Railroad would no longer accept transfer goods or passengers from the Central. A similar announcement from the New York and Harlem followed. Keep's desperate attempts to arrange alternate routes through New England were unfeasible. Central stock plunged, and since all of this happened before Keep and his group completed their selling, they suffered disastrous losses.

Vanderbilt quietly bought the depressed stock. After three days, during which goods piled up at Albany, unhappy stockholders pressured the Central board to make a deal with Vanderbilt. The deal soon followed, Central stock shot up and Vanderbilt came out on top of the heap again.

In 1867 a group that held almost half of the Central's stock petitioned Vanderbilt to become the president of the New York Central. He accepted, and soon almost all of the old guard were

gone, replaced by Vanderbilt men, including many family members. William H Vanderbilt was named vice-president.

While the Commodore was hardly altruistic, he did demonstrate more responsibility for the well-being of the roads under his control than men like Jay Gould and Jim Fisk. He did not hesitate to spend money on improvements when they were needed, and he took an active interest in the day-to-day running of the roads. However, he was well aware that his real expertise was Wall Street, and he left the operation of the railroad largely to William.

Vanderbilt's objective was a merger of the New York Central, the Hudson River and the New York and Harlem. He also had ideas of bringing in the Erie, but this objective eluded him. His failure to capture the Erie was one of the few cases in which his adversaries got the best of him, and one of the most spectacular battles of the 'Erie Wars.'

The Commodore started his campaign to gain control of the Erie in 1868, using the same tactics as before, that is, purchase of every share offered. At the time, Drew shared control of the Erie with Jay Gould and Jim Fisk, forming an unsavory trio called the 'Erie Ring.' Their reputations as unscrupulous scoun-

drels had been well earned. This trio of buccaneers printed 50,000 counterfeit Erie stock certificates, nearly all of which were bought by Vanderbilt. The plot was discovered, and a warrant for their arrest was issued. Always a step ahead of the law – and everyone else who was after them – they fled to New Jersey on a Hudson River ferry, with $6,000,000 in their luggage and the law and angry stockholders hot on their heels. In Jersey City they holed up in Taylor's Hotel, guarded by several hundred hired thugs armed with just about every weapon except Civil War cannons.

What followed could be called the 'Battle of the Bribes.' The Erie Ring knew what they had to do. Drew traveled to Albany, where he greased the palm of every legislator he could find in hope of inducing the legislature to pass a bill legalizing the bogus stock. However, Vanderbilt was able to buy more legislators, and the bill was defeated. At this point, Gould, in open defiance of the threat of arrest, appeared in Albany carrying a satchel filled with half a million dollars, with which he hoped to become an active participant in the legislative process. Before any lawmakers could benefit from the eloquent persuasive points in Gould's satchel, however, he was arrested and removed to New York City under the watchful eye of a sheriff. No one was too surprised when the sheriff, and Gould, still holding on to his satchel, turned up in Albany again. The sheriff announced that Gould was too sick to see anyone and would be held in an Albany hotel room. Despite his custodian's presence on guard at the door, somehow enough members of the State Senate were bought to pass the bill legalizing the stock.

Before the lower New York House got its share of the satchel, the adversaries arrived at a settlement. Drew bought back the shares from Vanderbilt at a reduced price, cutting the Commodore's losses to a few million. With these gains, the Erie Ring continued its financial piracy, ruining thousands along the way. Gould and Fisk continued their rape of the Erie, turning on Drew in the process; Vanderbilt's old adversary was left ragged and destitute. The Erie board of directors finally managed to oust Gould, and ordered his arrest for embezzlement, but the old pirate simply went West, where he continued his career of railroad ravaging, scheming to the hour of his death in 1892. Fisk left this world in more spectacular fashion, shot to death on the stairs of a New York hotel by a jealous rival for the affections of one Josie Mansfield, a would-be actress who had been Fisk's mistress.

Recovering quickly from the Erie debacle, the Commodore turned his attention to the merger of the New York Central and the Hudson River Railroads, which was completed in 1869. The result of the merger was called the New York Central and Hudson River Railroad. A huge stock-watering scheme engineered by Vanderbilt increased the paper value of the stock until the NYC and HR was capitalized at $45 million. The term 'stock watering' probably originated from one of Daniel Drew's favorite tricks during his days as a cattle dealer. Just before sale, he would give the stock salt blocks to lick. This made them drink large quantities of water, increasing their apparent weight.

Vanderbilt, always a lover of the grand and magnificent, then started construction of the grandest and most magnificent railroad depot the great city of New York had ever seen. Grand Central Depot, as it was first called, started to go up at Fourth Avenue and 42nd Streets in 1869. The site was that of the New York and Harlem Railroad's steam locomotive terminal. Critics said the 42nd Street location was too far north of the business district. However, the city was rapidly expanding northward, 42nd Street was a wide thoroughfare, newly paved with cobblestones, and it was the route of the new cross-town horse car. The decision was sealed by the city's prohibition against the operation of steam locomotives south of 42nd Street.

To accommodate the new depot, Vanderbilt acquired more land between Madison and Lexington Avenues up to 48th Street, and spent about $1 million on track construction that gave the NYC and HR access to this new terminal. The new track, con-structed along the east bank of the Harlem River and Spuyten Duyvil Creek, was called the Spuyten Duyvil and Port Morris Railroad. Vanderbilt found it to his advantage to lease this track to the NYC and HR; the lines were not legally merged until 1913.

Two years in construction at a cost of more than $3 million, the terminal was essentially a huge cylindrical train shed. It was 200 feet wide, 600 feet long and 100 feet in height at its highest point. Support was provided by 30 semicircular, elaborately decorated wrought iron trusses. Sections of glass ran along the domed roof. Twelve tracks were housed in the shed, ten of which terminated there, while two continued on to the old station at 27th Street.

The south and west sides of the structure were flanked by an L-shaped building which contained the waiting rooms, ticket offices and other passenger facilites. The north side, where the trains entered and departed, was enclosed by a curtain wall of steel and glass, which was actually nothing more than a false front.

Three railroads used Grand Central Depot: the New York Central and Hudson, the New York and Harlem, and the New York and New Haven. The latter was a tenant, and relations between tenant and landlord were not always amiable. The Vanderbilt railroads began to use the new terminal in 1871. The New Haven, however, unhappy about the rental fees, continued to move its trains south by horse to 27th Street for another year, until the dispute was resolved. The old 27th Street station was bought by P T Barnum, who later converted it into the first arena to be called Madison Square Garden. It is no small irony that the present Madison Square Garden is built on the site of Pennsylvania Station, the other great New York City terminal, built by the Pennsylvania Railroad. As the New York Central grew, so did its depot, which in later years came to be known as Grand Central Terminal.

William Vanderbilt's zeal to extend the Central to Chicago was not shared by the Commodore. Eventually, however, the elder Vanderbilt went along with his son's plans, carrying out the necessary financial manipulations at which he was so much more adept than William. The first step was to patch up the community of interests that Erastus Corning had arranged with the Lake Shore and the Michigan Central. The latter proved to be no problem, since its chairman, James Joy, who was on the Central Board, was amenable to co-operation and indicated that he would at least talk about a merger. The Lake Shore and Michigan Southern (formerly the Lake Shore), however, was quite another story. Acquiring this line was vital to establishing a Chicago connection, but it was run by men not at all friendly to

Opposite: William K Vanderbilt: the third generation.
Below: A 4-4-0 of the type used for fast mail runs.

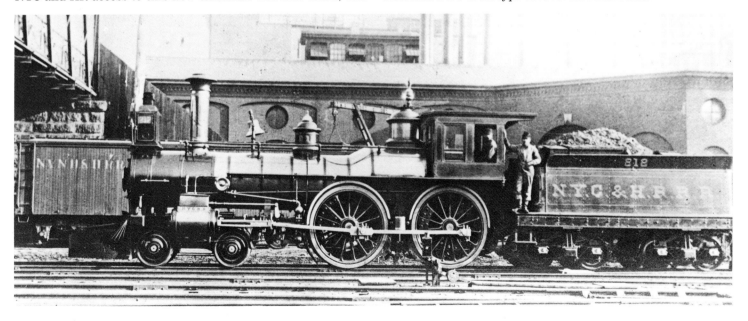

the Vanderbilts, including LeGrand Lockwood, who controlled the line, and Henry Keep, who was a large stockholder.

The Commodore tested the waters by buying a few shares and waited for the right time to make his move. He was inadvertently helped by Jay Gould and Jim Fisk, who in their 1869 attempt to corner the gold market had caused the financial ruin of thousands, including LeGrand Lockwood, who had to raise cash fast. Lockwood sold his railroad to Vanderbilt for the bargain price of $10 million. Vanderbilt's son-in-law, Horace Clark, was made president of the Lake Shore and Michigan Southern.

James Joy was more than willing to sell the Michigan Central, but perhaps sensing that he was in a seller's market, demanded a price the Vanderbilts thought excessive. The Michigan Central did eventually come into the field, but it did so share by share, helped along by the Panic of 1873, which sharply depressed the price of railroad shares. Full control was not obtained until 1878, and with that acquisition the New York-Chicago connection was complete.

The old Commodore did not live long enough to see the New York Central extend to Chicago. He died in 1877. A ragged and forlorn Daniel Drew showed up at the funeral. He may have been aware that with the Commodore's passing, and his own fall into obscurity, an era had come to an end. From this time on there would be few places for rough-and-tumble, tobacco-chewing hayseeds like himself and the Commodore in American enterprise. The future now belonged to J P Morgan and others like him, who were forging a new brand of capitalism.

William Vanderbilt turned to Morgan several times during his tenure as president of the Central. In 1879 he asked Morgan to sell more than 60 percent of the shares he held, but to do it quietly so there would be no panic. Morgan agreed, but asked a high price. In addition to a commission of $1 million, Morgan wanted a guarantee that the dividend would remain at 8 percent, and that he or one of his men would have a seat on the Central board. Vanderbilt agreed, and thus began the Morgan Age of American railroading. The Vanderbilts gradually became less important to the Central, and Morgan became the dominant figure – not only in the Central, but in all American railroads.

Starting in 1882, William Vanderbilt expanded the Central westward. He leased the bankrupt Canada Southern and merged it with the Michigan Central. Then he moved southward into the Pennsylvania Railroad's territory through acquisitions of the

Pittsburgh and Lake Erie and a number of small lines. The biggest event of that year for William was getting the New York, Chicago, and St Louis Railroad (the Nickel Plate Road), a move that extended the Central to St Louis. William was on the Union Pacific board, and for a while he gave some thought to acquiring that line. Had he done so, the United States would have had a coast-to-coast railroad. Of course, the Pennsylvania did not sit back and let William have his way. They responded by moving into Central territory and cutting their rates, thus starting a chaotic period in American railroad history.

William resigned from the presidency in 1883. However, he retained seats on the boards of various constituent lines. He made his son Cornelius II chairman of the New York Central and the Michigan Central, while another son, William K, was given the chairmanship of the Lake Shore and Michigan Southern. The elder Vanderbilt was well aware of his offsprings' limitations, so he named James Rutter as the president and chief operating officer of the New York Central (Rutter had previously been general traffic manager). When he died soon after taking office, Vanderbilt, who had suffered a stroke, named Chauncey M Depew as the Central's chief executive officer. Depew did not

know a great deal about railroads, but he was a skillfull politician and was on good terms with the powers in Washington. The actual running of the railroad was left to technicians.

From the time it became an entity in the mid 1850s, the New York Central had no serious competition in New York. The Erie tried, but had never been able to mount a challenge of any consequence. Through the 1860s and 1870s, various groups of entrepreneurs tried to organize competing lines. While many of these obtained charters, their progress was limited to surveying routes and laying a few miles of track before they went bust.

The situation changed in the 1880s, when the Central found itself in fierce competition with the Pennsylvania; for the first time, the prospect of a competing line in New York was very real indeed. In 1880 a strongly financed group took over the assets of the New York, West Shore and Chicago, one of the failed would-be competitors of the Central, renaming it the New York, West Shore and Buffalo. Among the investors was George Pullman, still seething over the Central's decision to use Webster Wag-

Lake Shore and Michigan Southern express along Lake Erie.

ner's sleeping cars instead of his and intent upon revenge. Closely allied with a group of bankers who organized something called the North Shore Railroad, the new operation was generally called the West Shore, because it was projected to run along the west shore of the Hudson River. By 1883 the West Shore had constructed tracks from Jersey City to Newburgh and from there to Albany and Syracuse. Limited operations started that same year, and the Central immediately put on the pressure by cutting rates. The West Shore was soon in deep trouble, declaring bankruptcy in 1884.

Wall Street brokers were quite surprised when sales of the bankrupt West Shore's stock continued to be brisk. The buyer was George Roberts, president of the Pennsylvania Railroad, who hoped to revive the West Shore and show the Central what it was like to have real competition. This move plunged the two railroad giants into a rate war that came in the middle of an economic depression and would have been disastrous had it continued. J P Morgan was deeply disturbed by this corporate mayhem, fearing that the entire structure of American capitalism could be irreversibly damaged. He wanted what amounted to a peace conference, but Chauncey Depew would do nothing without the approval of Vanderbilt, who was on an extended vacation in Europe. So Morgan went to Europe to fetch Vanderbilt, and they returned on the same ship.

The peace conference was held in July of 1885 aboard Morgan's yacht *Corsair*. It was reported that Morgan chose the yacht as the site so no one could storm out in anger. In attendance were George Roberts, Frank Thomson (who would become president of the Pennsylvania in 1897), Chauncey Depew and Morgan. The four men settled down in deck chairs, and as the *Corsair* sailed up and down the Hudson, they drank Morgan's whiskey and hammered out their agreement. The Pennsylvania agreed to sell off its West Shore stock, which would be bought by a group headed by Morgan and Depew, who would lease the line to the New York Central. Vanderbilt agreed to sell his shares in the South Pennsylvania Railroad, a line that had been started to compete with the Pennsylvania. He also agreed to give up his interest in the Reading Railroad, which competed sharply with the Pennsylvania for coal-hauling business.

With the *Corsair* agreement, Morgan consolidated his position as the most powerful financier in the country and the enforcer of order in the railroad industry. The Central and the Pennsylvania continued to be rivals, but they found that with Morgan tightly in control of the purse, there was little they could do without his tacit approval. The Interstate Commerce Commission (ICC) had been established in 1877 to enforce various federal railroad regulations, which were largely ignored in the late nineteenth century. The real regulating force was Morgan. For example, in 1894 the Central and Pennsylvania worked out an agreement for pooling freight business and for consultation on rates and matters of expansion into each other's territory. This was in violation of all kinds of federal regulations. However, because Morgan approved of the agreement, the ICC did nothing.

Agreements of this kind ran counter to the spirit of capitalism, but true competition was proving to be more than railroads could cope with. Most European Governments had recognized this situation and were nationalizing their railroads, turning them into governmental services. Nationalizing of industries was and continues to be anathema to most Americans. In the past, men like J P Morgan provided the order that nationalization provided elsewhere. But when the Morgans had gone, chaos returned, and railroads were unable to stand up to the pressures of competition.

Below: A Civil War-era 'Buffalo' switcher and its crew.

Opposite: The north end of Grand Central Depot as seen from the yards in 1883.

ccording to the New York Central's annual report of 1870, the railroad had 740 miles of track, of which 666.5 miles were double tracked. There were 408 locomotives, 445 passenger cars, 132 baggage cars and 9026 freight cars in operation. Over the next ten years, locomotives and rolling stock were added as needed to accommodate increasing traffic. While passenger traffic increased some 15 percent over this period, and ton-miles of freight almost tripled, there had been little change in track mileage. Consequently , the Central was hard pressed to keep things running smoothly and safely.

Accidents were frequent, but it seems remarkable that they were not daily events. If, for example, a train stalled because of mechanical problems, the engineer of an approaching train would have no way of knowing it was there until he saw it. If the stalled train was on a curve, the sighting might be too late.

One of the worst accidents on the Central occurred on the night of 6 February 1871. A train called the Pacific Express left the old Hudson River Railroad Station at Ninth Avenue and Thirtieth Street on schedule at 8:00 PM. As the train entered a drawbridge over Wappinger's Creek, near New Hamburgh, the engineer of the passenger train saw that a freight train on the opposite track was derailing; wreckage piling up and spilling over onto the other track made a collision imminent. The engineer knew he would not be able to stop in time to avoid plowing into the wreckage. The fireman jumped off, but the engineer remained in the cab, still trying to stop, and was killed. The freight train was mostly tank cars, and fire broke out on impact. The forward cars of the passenger train were ablaze almost immediately, killing everyone in the first sleeper. The fire spread quickly to the next cars in line, but their occupants were able to escape. Some fast-thinking passengers uncoupled cars not yet burning and pushed them away from the wreckage. Twenty-two people were killed.

Of course, accidents did nothing to improve the Central's public image. Whenever there was an accident, newspapers were quick to attack the railroad. The usual target of the attacks was William Vanderbilt, who had to contend with a bad press for much of his life. His coarse,loutish appearance and his copious bushy sideburns made him a favorite subject of newspaper cartoonists. One of his more unfortunate utterances was the now-famous 'The public be damned!' He is supposed to have made the statement in 1882 in answer to a question from a reporter about the Central's duty to the public. The statement was widely quoted, although it seems it was taken out of context and Vanderbilt did not mean exactly what the words implied.

To remain competitive, the Central had to increase both the speed of passenger trains and the volume of freight traffic without jeopardizing safety. Vanderbilt's solution was to four-track the line between Albany and Buffalo. This work started in 1873 and proceeded smoothly until the following summer, when the Central ran into determined opposition from some farmers near the town of Port Byron.

In most cases, the railroad was able to buy the land needed for

Previous pages: *The Albany terminal, a vital nerve center for the Central, where switchers like this 0-4-0 were in constant use.*

Left: Harper's Weekly *woodcut depicting a fatal collision near Steamburg, New York, in 1888.*
Opposite: *William H Vanderbilt, who extended the Central's empire before the century turned.*

track expansion. If any landowners along the way resisted sell-ing, laws allowed the railroad to force sale through a condemna-tion process. The Port Byron farmers announced that they would defy the state's order to sell, and physically resist the Central's track-laying gangs. They erected a barricade of logs and earth, and raised an 'army' of 50 well-armed locals to defend it. The superintendent in charge of construction gathered his own army of railroad employees and transported them to the rebellion site in a special train. He then ordered what amounted to a frontal attack against the barricade. The railroad employees wisely refused to obey the order. Many had fought in the Civil War, and they were not about to die for their railroad at the 'Battle of Port Byron.' The infuriated superintendent fired them all on the spot. The matter was eventually settled in the courts, but the superintendent stubbornly refused to rehire any of the reluctant warriors.

Pitched battles between rival railroad gangs were not uncom-mon in the West at this time, but fighting was not a usual job requirement for employees of the Central. However, working for the Central or any other railroad was not at all a soft job. Life on the railroad could be particularly hard during times of economic downturn. There were no laws limiting the number of hours an employee could be required to work. Doubling up of shifts was common, and many employees welcomed the chance to earn extra money. An engineeer doing double shifts could earn almost $200 a month, which was a fair amount of money in the mid 1870s. A brakeman earned about $50 a month, and a con-ductor drew about $60 – more, if he were not entirely honest. Many conductors profited from unticketed passengers who paid

their fares on the train. There was no system at the time to keep a conductor from pocketing the fare.

Railroad work was dangerous, and few lines had programs of compensation for widows and orphans of workers killed on the job. A magnanimous railroad owner might give a widow a few dollars and a sympathetic pat on the hand. Brakemen and cou-plers seemed to have the shortest life expectancy. In the early days, coupling was done by a worker standing between the cars, who dropped a metal pin into the coupling mechanism as the cars rolled into contact. Mangled or missing arms and hands were the mark of the coupler. Brakemen were more likely to be killed outright than maimed, since their main hazard was fall-ing off moving trains.

The New York Central seems to have had fewer labor problems and more loyal employees than most other railroads in the East. The Erie, on the other hand, was almost done in by strikes. The Central suffered far less in the Great Railway Strike of 1877 than did most other railroads. The strike was a legacy of the Panic of 1873, which resulted in a lingering Depression and widespread unemployment. Most railroads continued to pay dividends to stockholders, but they cut back on maintenance and wages. In the past, railroad workers had accepted the cuts, knowing bitterly that there was little they could do about it. By the 1870s, however, the labor movement was beginning to grow. Most unions were not yet strong enough to mount a serious challenge to management, but there were plenty of unemployed men available to stage massive protest demonstrations. More than 20,000 demonstrated in Chicago on a cold day in December of 1873. The following month, police charged into a huge labor

Opposite, below: *Accidents became frequent when the speed and volume of traffic outstripped safety measures.*

Brakemen were particularly liable to injury and even death in falls from moving trains, as seen in this Harper's Weekly cartoon: an applicant for the position is told that there have been no fatalities this week.

PRESIDENT (*to anxious Applicant for a situation as Brakeman*). "Want a berth, eh!—(*to Book-keeper*)—Mr. JONES, has there been a Brakeman killed on the road within a day or two?"
Mr. JONES. "Well, no, Sir, none this week."
PRESIDENT (*to Applicant*). "Ah! well, my man, call next Monday, and by that time I guess there'll be a vacancy."

rally in New York, swinging their clubs and bloodying hundreds of heads.

In June of 1877, the Pennsylvania Railroad announced a wage cut of 10 percent. Other roads followed, including the New York Central and its satellites, the Erie, and the Baltimore and Ohio. Most railroad employees resigned themselves to the cuts as before. However, B&O firemen and brakemen filed a formal protest with management, which listened politely and retained the cuts. On that same day, firemen in Martinsburg, West Virginia, climbed down from their locomotives and refused to work. Earlier that day, forty firemen in Baltimore had been fired for doing the same thing. Things were different in Martinsburg. Crowds prevented the police from arresting the strikers. The brakemen joined the firemen, and two days later some 70 stalled trains blocked all traffic at this important junction. The governor sent out the militia, but since most of the militiamen were friends and relatives of the strikers, they did nothing to hinder the strike. The governor then proposed to personally lead a militia unit from another city into the strikers, but changed his mind when he learned that support for the strike was growing. He then asked President Rutherford B Hayes for federal troops. Hayes obliged, and in a few days federal regulars began to move trains out through a gauntlet of hostile, jeering strikers and sympathizers.

The strike spread to other sections of the B&O, prompting the governor of Maryland to call out the troops, many of whom soon found themselves in great peril. At Camden Junction, units of the Maryland militia were surrounded by a mob of more than 2000, who threw stones at them. The militia fired into the mob, killing 10 and wounding many more. Again, the federals were called in, and they came in force, equipped for full-scale battle. The B&O management refused to negotiate with the strikers and with the help of massive numbers of federal troops, the strike was broken. But the rest of the American railroad industry would pay dearly for the obstinancy of the B&O.

On 19 July 1877, employees of the Pennsylvania Railroad left their engines at Pittsburgh when they heard of the B&O strike. Again, the local militia did nothing, but a troop of 1000 men from Philadelphia fired into the crowd, killing 20 and wounding many more, including women and children.

What followed made many observers think a revolution, if not the Apocalypse, had descended upon the United States of America. After the shooting, the troops retreated to a roundhouse that was soon surrounded by 15,000 outraged, shrieking men and women, many of whom were armed. Three soldiers who tried to flee the roundhouse were shot down as they ran. Some of the mob poured oil into a coal-filled gondola, set it afire and rammed it into the roundhouse. The terrified troops came charging out, shooting an escape route through the crowd.

Fire broke out in lines of freight cars standing outside of Pittsburgh's Union Depot. It spread to destroy hundreds of locomotives and cars, the depot, the Union Hotel, the Pennsylvania Railroad offices and other buildings. It was a disaster as great as the burning of Atlanta and other Civil War calamities, but to many, the Pittsburgh uprising was nothing less than war.

The strike spread to the Erie and the New York Central. Cen-

NOCK, President.
LAWTON, Treasurer.
STRYKER, Secretary.

NEW YORK LOCOMOTIVE WORKS.
ROME, N. Y.

New York Office:
34½ PINE STREET

tral employees walked off the job in a number of cities, including Rochester and Syracuse. Some freight trains were stopped, but passenger trains were allowed to pass, and there was no property damage. It seemed like a company picnic compared to what was going on elsewhere. When William Vanderbilt was interviewed by the press, he calmly stated that he had no knowledge of any strike on the Central. Within a week the whole thing was over, and the men were back at work.

How did the Central get off so painlessly, while the Pennsylvania and others were nearly destroyed? A very important factor was that on the Central the wage cut applied to everybody, including executives. This was not the case on most of the other roads affected by the strike. Vanderbilt made grand public statements to the effect that the cuts would be rescinded 'the moment that the business of the country will justify it.' He then announced that a bonus of $100,000 was to be divided among the loyal employees. This was a rare coup in public relations on his part. The $100,000 was nothing to a man with a personal fortune exceeding $200 million, but giving it away made him seem like a benevolent master who really cared about his workers. Most significantly, Vanderbilt agreed to negotiate with the strikers. Half of the wage cut was restored on 1 July 1877, and the balance early in 1880. Vanderbilt bought peace on the Central even as the strike violence spread westward to Chicago.

Opposite, top: *The late nineteenth century saw dramatic advances in the design of locomotives like this 0-6-0 of 1889.*
Opposite, bottom: *The Lake Shore and Michigan Southern Ticonderoga – a 4-4-0 type widely used for mixed traffic.*
Below: *Ten percent wage cuts precipitated this 1877 strike by Baltimore & Ohio workmen in Martinsburg, West Virginia. Federal troops failed to keep the strike from spreading.*

1877 was just not a good year for railroads. While the Central did not suffer much inconvenience from the strike, it was paralyzed by the great blizzard of that winter. Ironically, it was the new four-track system that caused much of the trouble. Existing plows could handle two tracks reasonably well, but all they could accomplish on four was to push the snow from one track to another. In New York City, the weight of snow on the glass roof of the Grand Central trainshed caused a section of the roof to collapse, showering the platforms with glass, snow and iron. Fortunately, the station was almost empty, and no one was injured.

The collapse of the roof was only the beginning of a series of troubles relating to the depot. For one thing, it was inadequate almost from the moment it was finished. Attempts to expand were always met with determined opposition by New Yorkers, who were growing tired of smoke-belching locomotives rolling down some of their more fashionable streets. The trainshed itself was remarkably free of smoke and fumes, due to a unique system of arrivals and departures. Locomotives for outbound trains were kept out of the shed until just before departure time, when they were backed up and coupled to the train. The arrival procedure was much more spectacular and a source of great fascination for the passengers. Just after passing an upgrade at 49th Street, the engineer would shut off steam and a brakeman would release the coupling mechanism. The engineer would then pour on the steam to pull away from the train, parting the air-brake hose connection with a loud hiss and snap. The locomotive would proceed down a track off to the side, while the train rolled into the station by grace of its inertia; there brakemen slowed it to a stop on the platform.

What particularly concerned citizens of New York was that the tracks from upper Manhattan into Grand Central were laid

on grade level along Fourth (now Park) Avenue. This was indeed a dangerous situation, and there were many accidents. The Central did not improve its relations with the locals by building a yard that extended north to 49th Street and west to Madison Avenue. There was constant movement of switch engines in the yard, and anyone trying to cross the complex of tracks did so at his own peril. The situation became a grand cause for newspapers. The general demand was for the Central to sink the tracks below street level — an expensive undertaking which the Central was not too eager to begin. Encouraged, perhaps, by the possibility that the legislature would pass a bill compelling the Central to lower its tracks, Vanderbilt agreed, but not before getting the city to bear half the cost. Construction started in 1872 and the project took two years to complete.

The lowering of the tracks started at 45th Street, since all agreed that doing so right at the terminal was impractical. An open cut with foot bridges was constructed as far as 56th Street. From 56th north to 67th Street, what was called a 'beam tunnel'

was built. This consisted of a double-tracked center tunnel running down the center of Fourth Avenue, provided with sizeable ventilation rectangles spanned by iron beams. The open tunnel was flanked by single-tracked closed tunnels. The result was considered quite attractive. The ventilation rectangles were enclosed by wrought iron fences and the areas around the openings were planted in trees and shrubs, giving Fourth Avenue a park-like aspect. Fourth Avenue, now generally called Park Avenue, was widened to accommodate a 27-foot carriageway and a 15-foot sidewalk on either side of the landscaped carriage openings. The smoke chuffing out of the openings, only to disappear as the locomotive went under the cross streets, must have been a fascinating sight.

From 67th to 71st Streets the tunnel was fully enclosed.

Below: *The 2-8-0 wheel arrangement was a standard for freight locomotives.*

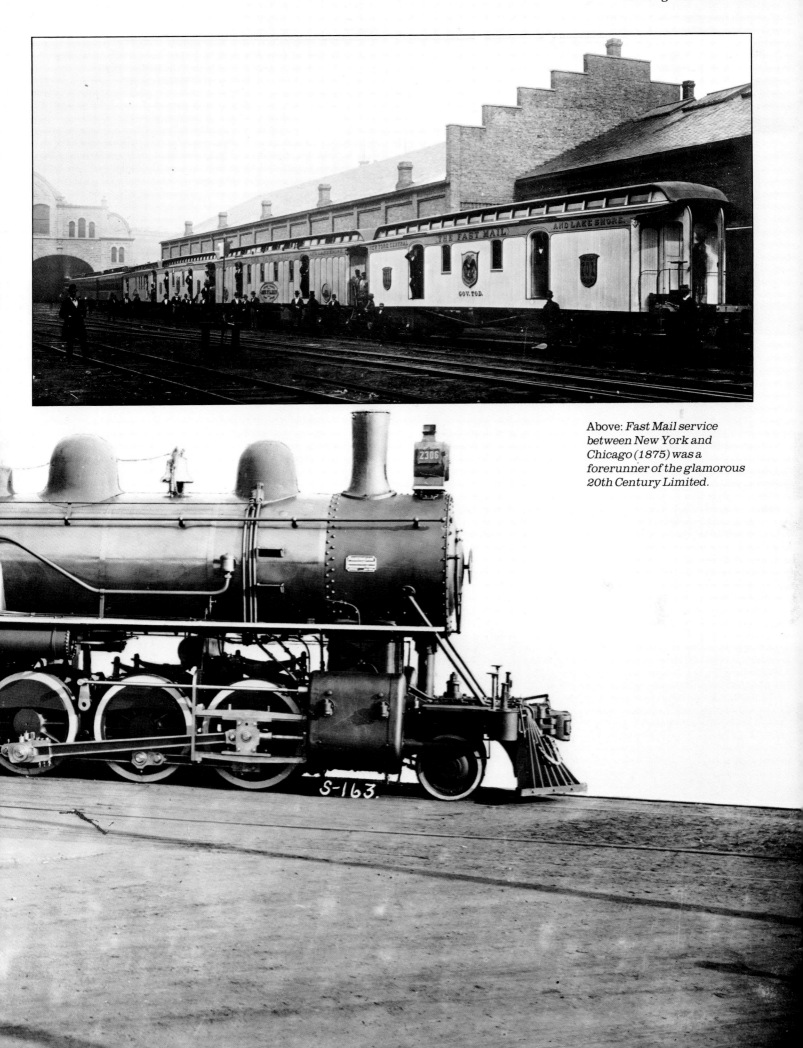

Above: *Fast Mail service between New York and Chicago (1875) was a forerunner of the glamorous 20th Century Limited.*

Another beam tunnel carried the tracks to 80th Street, and from 80th to 98th Street the tunnel was fully enclosed again. From 98th Street to 115th Street there was a stone viaduct, and beyond that point the tracks ran in an open depressed cut to the Harlem River.

Once his grand palace of a depot was finished, and the New York Central had been four-tracked to Buffalo, the Commodore turned his attention to developing high-speed trains. One of the fastest locomotives in the Central fleet was the 110, or Flying Devil. Built in 1874 in the Central's Syracuse shop, the locomotive had 17-inch cylinders with a 24-inch stroke. The wheels of this 4-4-0 locomotive (a coal-burner) were slightly over six feet in diameter. The Flying Devil reached speeds of 60mph pulling the Commodore's private car *Duchess* over straight stretches in western New York. This engine was used for one of the Central's first high-speed trains soon after it was built.

Vanderbilt decided to try a special Sunday-only New York-Chicago service. The first of these trains pulled out of Grand Central on 4 July 1875. From New York to Albany, the small train (two baggage cars and a coach) was pulled by Engine Number 70. At Albany, 110 took over. It left Albany at 6:00 AM and was scheduled to pull into Buffalo at 1:00 PM the same day. Those who knew about these things said it couldn't be done. They predicted hot boxes and all kinds of other troubles, not the least of which was the possibility of derailment. The train got into Buffalo at 12:55 PM. There were no hot boxes, no derailments, and 110 reached 75mph on some of the straight stretches. The train, pulled by another engine, went on to Chicago, arriving there at 8:00 AM Monday morning – on schedule.

At about the same time the Central introduced its fast New York-Chicago train, the superintendent of the Post Office's Railway Mail Service, George S Bangs, went to the Commodore with an interesting proposition. Bangs had convinced the Post Office of the feasibility of running a 24-hour mail service between New York and Chicago, and he wanted to know if Vanderbilt would be interested in taking the contract for it. The Central would have to adhere to the schedule and to build 20 special cars for the mail train. The Commodore was not at all interested, so Banks went to his son, William. Apparently, the younger Vanderbilt was easier to convince; he made a deal with Bangs. The Commodore did not try to stop the contract, but he did warn his son of the pitfalls of dealing with the Federal Government.

The first Fast Mail left Grand Central on 14 September 1875. It was, without doubt, the most beautiful train the United States had ever seen, painted white with buff stripes and gold trim. The sides bore the Great Seal of the United States and the Post Office emblem. The train met its schedule despite the need to make meal stops for the dignitaries who rode in the Commodore's private car. After the first trip, the Fast Mail provided no passenger service.

The Fast Mail was an immediate success. Clerks sorted the mail right on the train, an innovation that had only recently been introduced. However, less than a year after its inauguration, Congress reduced the rates paid to railroads for carrying the mails. Just how emphatic the Commodore's 'I told you so' was is not known. The service was discontinued, and a disheartened Bangs resigned from the Post Office. His successor persuaded Congress to make new appropriations, and the service was resumed in 1877, not only on the New York Central, but on several other lines as well.

The Fast Mail excited the imagination of the public. Songs and plays were written about these trains, which picked up the mail from stanchions along the track as they moved past. The mail trains served to prove that fast train service was feasible. Their success led to the service that would be regarded as the finest achievement of the New York Central – The Twentieth Century Limited.

Below: *New York, New Haven & Hartford trains in 1889.*

Opposite: *Reconstruction work on the Grand Central Depot, 1900.*

In the last 20 years of the nineteenth century, William H Vanderbilt actively sought to expand the Central through the acquisition of other lines. Shortly after the West Shore threat was removed, Vanderbilt bought the Cleveland, Cincinnati, Chicago and St Louis – a line generally known as the Big Four. It was a sizeable enterprise, and its acquisition extended the Central south from Chicago into southern Illinois. Smaller additions to the Central fold included the Beech Creek, a 153-mile line running from the New Jersey shore to Clearfield, Pennsyvania. This line so worried the Pennsylvania Railroad that it tried to sabotage the track construction by dropping an old locomotive down a ravine onto the right-of-way.

The Rome, Watertown, and Ogdensburg was added in 1891. Prior to this purchase, the Central had made plans for expanding into Watertown, New York; surveyors had already been sent out. This line enabled the Central to connect with Canada's Grand Trunk Railway for access to Montreal.

The biggest addition of the late nineteenth century was the Boston and Albany. Although the line was not purchased outright, it came under total control of the Central in 1894. New Englanders were not at all happy about the loss of 'their' railroad to the New Yorkers. William H ('the public be damned') Vanderbilt was not noted for his tact, and he promptly added outrage to the New Englander's indignation by having New York Central logos painted on the Boston and Albany rolling stock. Newspapers were filled with angry editorials, poets composed odes of protest and there was talk of a boycott. Vanderbilt gave in and had the hated words 'New York Central' removed from all rolling stock sent east of New York's borders.

The world-famous
EMPIRE STATE EXPRESS
leads this fast fleet of
11 trains to BUFFALO

New York Central is now operating in its New York-Buffalo service the greatest fleet of fast trains ever seen on this popular route.

By day this is the scenic way through the historic Hudson and Mohawk Valleys—one of the world's most famous highways. At night it is a route of amazing comfort, because it is nearly at sea level all the way across New York State.

Every traveler to the West knows that "you can sleep on the water level route" of the New York Central. The fast overnight expresses give no feeling of high speed because the seasoned roadbed is so smooth and level.

One of the most popular day trains to upstate cities is the *Day Coach De Luxe* with its special type of luxurious coaches, and its wicker-chaired Observation Car without extra charge.

From Buffalo eastward there are 13 fast trains daily, arriving in New York between the hours of 6:10 a.m. and 11:45 p.m.

DAY SERVICE	
Empire State Ex.	8:30 a.m. 5:15 p.m.
Chicago Express	8:45 a.m. 7:15 p.m.
DayCoachDeLuxe	9:30 a.m. 8:00 p.m.
The Mohawk	11:00 a.m. 9:00 p.m.
NorthShore Ltd.	12:10 p.m. 9:40 p.m.
The Seneca	12:25 p.m. 10:15 p.m.

Dining Car on All Day Trains
(All Schedules Standard Time)

OVERNIGHT SERVICE	
	Lv. NewYork Ar. Buffalo
WesternExpress*	6:10 p.m. 6:40 a.m.
The Niagara	8:35 p.m. 7:05 a.m.
Buffalonian**	9:30 p.m. 8:10 a.m.
The Iroquois**	11:20 p.m. 8:20 a.m.
The Genesee**	11:35 p.m. 9:50 a.m.

*Dining Car Serving Dinner
**Dining Car Serving Breakfast

New York Central

THE WATER LEVEL ROUTE   YOU CAN SLEEP

For reservations telephone   VANderbilt 3200

It was now clear to the people who ran the New York Central that the age of public relations had arrived. They needed someone to help improve the Central's public image, and that someone was George H Daniels, the Central's passenger agent. A short, plump man sporting a white goatee, Daniels bombarded the Central management with ideas from the moment he was hired. Daniels convinced the Central managers to run a special New York-Buffalo train to be called the Empire State Express. A special big-wheeled, Atlantic-type locomotive was constructed just to haul this train. On 14 September 1891, the 436-mile run from New York to Buffalo was made in seven hours and six minutes, including stops, at an average speed of 61.4mph. This was a new record.

New record or not, Daniels was not satisfied with the performance. He ordered a new engine – 999 – and planned to show her off at the 1893 Chicago World's Fair. On 10 May 1893, engineer Charlie Hogan climbed into 999's cab at Syracuse to take the throttle for the last leg of the trip into Buffalo. All that is certain is that on a straight section of track near Batavia the train went very fast indeed: New York Central publicists claimed that for one mile, 999 traveled at a speed of 112.5mph. Some years later, there were 'confessions' that the speed had been only 90mph. However, even that figure was record-breaking for the time.

Whatever the true speed, Daniels got all the publicity mileage he could out of 999. She made the run to Chicago pulling a train Daniels called the Exposition Flyer. It reached the city in 20 hours and was put on display at the Chicago World's Fair with a replica of the DeWitt Clinton. Daniels then convinced the Postmaster General to issue a two-cent stamp commemorating the Empire State Express. The picture of the train on the stamp was skillfully drawn to suggest speed. Several years thereafter, Daniels attracted attention by giving a copy of Elbert Hubbard's *A Message to Garcia* to all passengers on New York Central trains. This little book, about a man who heroically delivers a message from Theodore Roosevelt to a Cuban insurgent general hiding in the jungle, appealed to the patriotic fervor generated by the Spanish-American War.

Daniels's tour-de-force came at the opening of the new century. He wanted to run the fastest, most luxurious train in the country on the Central's New York-Chicago route. He could have continued to call the train the Empire State Express, but he wanted a new name to evoke the idea of continuing progress into the new century, so he chose to call it the Twentieth Century. Shortly thereafter, when it was decided to limit the number of stops, the name was altered to the Twentieth Century Limited.

Twentieth Century Limited service started in 1902. The Century was scheduled to make the 960-mile run to Chicago in 20 hours, for an average speed of 80mph. Again, there were those who said it couldn't be done: dashing a souped-up locomotive down a short stretch of track at foolhardy speeds for a minute or two was one thing, they pointed out, but maintaining daily high-speed service was quite another. They predicted disastrous derailments and ripping-up of tracks and roadbed.

Daniels knew the track could take the punishment. Its soundness was not due to his publicity, but to the skill of Plimmon H Dudley, the Central's consulting engineer on rails. Dudley invented a device that could detect minute irregularities in the track. He designed a new type of rail that was significantly stronger than track previously used, but only about 20 percent heavier. Broken rails were dramatically reduced. The Central provided Dudley with a special car for his work; it contained Dudley's laboratory and an apartment that was home to him and his wife for more than 40 years. Without Dudley's improved track, there would have been no Twentieth Century Limited.

Daniels planned the Century as a train for wealthy and important people who required speed, demanded luxury and could pay for both. The train was scheduled to arrive in New York at 9:30

Previous pages: *A phalanx of streamlined Hudsons.*
Left: *A 1930s advertisement.*

Opposite: *George H Daniels, the Central's able passenger agent cum public-relations man.*

AM, allowing businessmen a full day's work, and pleasure travelers time for a taxi to the docks to board trans-Atlantic liners. The train was to be all-Pullman. By the turn of the century, the Wagner Palace Car Company, which had been closely allied with the Vanderbilts, had been absorbed by Pullman. The use of his cars on the crack train of the railroad that had snubbed him for so many years must have been a source of gloating satisfaction to Pullman. Passengers would sleep in their own roomettes and dine in the recently introduced dining car. They could avail themselves of a barber shop, a beauty salon, secretarial services, telephone and telegraph.

The Pennsylvania Railroad had been running its own fast train from New York to Chicago, the Pennsylvania Limited, for several years when Daniels started the Century. The Pennsylvania immediately upgraded its New York-Chicago service to make it competitive with the Central's, inaugurating a luxury, high-speed train between these two great cities that came to be called the Broadway Limited.

The competition between the Century and the Broadway became the most celebrated rivalry in the history of North American railroads. They kept pace with each other in matters of service, speed and luxury, with the major difference lying in the nature of the route. The Broadway's route was more direct, but went through some fairly mountainous terrain. The Central's route described a 90-degree angle — due north to Albany, then due west to Chicago — with the main line going through the relatively flat terrain of the Hudson and Mohawk Valleys and the Great Lakes shore, a circumstance that fostered use of the term 'Water Level Route' in the Central's advertising. The implication was that the Central's level route would provide passengers with a more comfortable ride and a better night's sleep.

Competition between the two trains was keen but not cutthroat. Both railroads considered their crack trains a source of pride, prestige and publicity. For a while, the schedules of the two trains were such that they were on parallel tracks a few miles outside of Chicago. This juxtaposition gave every appearance of a race, and many excited passengers believed the trains were indeed racing. Actually, their running times were kept equal by agreement between the competitors. As the Central and the Pennsylvania poured more money into these trains, they ceased to be moneymakers, but management justified their continuance as the best advertising money could buy.

Over the years, both the speed and the amenities of the Century were constantly improved. The first Century consisted of three sleepers, a diner and a library-buffet car. Later versions included cars with drawing rooms. The train became so popular that it was run in several sections, the wooden cars being replaced by all-steel equipment between 1910 and 1912. By the mid 1920s, the Central was calling the train a 'national institution,' and it had, in fact, become a source of patriotic pride. In 1912 the Pennsylvania and the Central agreed to a running time of 20 hours (the Central had previously made the run in 18 hours). In 1932 the two roads agreed to a time of 18 hours, and in 1935 it was reduced to 16.5 hours. The 18-hour time was cause for a celebration on the departure platform attended by Jimmy Walker, the flamboyant Mayor of New York, and William K Vanderbilt (a lesser force in Central affairs since 1903).

In the 1920s the Atlantics were replaced by big 4-6-4 locomotives called Hudsons; these hauled the Century until they were replaced by diesels in the 1950s. Modified over the years, the most powerful versions of the Hudson devloped more than 4700 horsepower at 75mph. The most noticeable change came in 1938 with the streamlined Hudson designed by Henry Dreyfuss. Actually, this locomotive was essentially the same old Hudson covered with what one observor called 'an upside-down bathtub.' Streamlining was supposed to cut down on air resistance and evoke an image of progress. The only certain thing about streamlining steam locomotives was that it covered many of the parts, making maintenance more difficult.

Arrivals and departures of the Century came to be as exciting as those of trans-Atlantic liners. A red carpet rolled out from the gate to the platform was the Central's way of telling the passengers they were special and could look forward to regal treatment in exchange for their extra fare. Many of the passengers were very special indeed. Celebrity hounds haunted the departure-gate area in hope of seeing such notables of the day as Kate Smith, Gloria Swanson and other movie stars, politicians, sports figures and others.

Century pasengers could enjoy such luxuries as fresh sole and

The Central set new speed records in the early twentieth century.

strawberries for breakfast. Before breakfast a newspaper appeared under their doors, and as they entered the dining car a boutonniere was presented to them. Wrinkled trousers or skirts were pressed by the valet — who doubled as the train secretary. There was a small group of zealots who regularly rode the Century just to get a shave and a haircut — a form of dandyism that entered popular legend.

The Twentieth Century Limited was the inspiration for songs, plays and radio shows. The Columbia Broadcasting System's 'Grand Central Station' was one of the most successful radio shows ever produced, for more than 20 years. In the 1940s and 1950s, millions of Americans did not consider their Saturday mornings to be complete until they had heard the famous opening:

As a bullet seeks its target, shining rails in every part of our great nation are aimed at Grand Central Station, heart of the country's greatest city. Drawn by the magnetic force of the fantastic metropolis, day and night great trains rush toward the Hudson River . . . then dive with a roar into the two-and-a-half mile tunnel beneath the glitter and swank of Park Avenue, and then — GRAND CENTRAL STATION! — crossroads of a million private lives, gigantic stage on which are played a thousand dramas daily.

Although no one seemed to care, the dramatic call of 'Grand Central Station!' was inaccurate. Since 1913 this midtown-New York landmark has been called Grand Central Terminal. By whatever name, Grand Central's history has been characterized by the need for constant improvements and additions to keep pace with its volume of traffic.

By the turn of the century, the New York Central and the City of New York had spent millions on sinking the Park Avenue tracks below street level and on other improvements. However, many New Yorkers still felt that the railroad was an unbearable intrusion into their lives. The yards still existed at ground level from 42nd to 56th Street, creating not only a safety hazard, but a smoky, grimy eyesore that was retarding the city's development. Existing tracks and switches in the yard and trainshed could not handle the volume of traffic. Trains often had to wait in the Park Avenue beam tunnel, spewing smoke all over citizens taking their strolls or carriage rides, and covering buildings in a film of soot.

The Central managers were also concerned about the effect of smoke and fumes on their operations. Often, the fumes were so thick that signals were obscured. The inevitable happened on 8 January 1902, when a New York Central train ran past a red signal and crashed into the rear of a standing New Haven train, killing 15 passengers. The need to do something about this situation was made all the more imperative by the response of the New York State Legislature to this tragedy. An act was passed prohibiting operation of steam locomotives south of the Harlem River after 1 July 1908. It was now up to the Central to figure out how they were going to get their trains into Grand Central after that date.

The solution to the Central's problems had been demonstrated as early as 1879, when the Siemens Company displayed a small electric locomotive at an exhibition in Berlin. In 1885 the Richmond Union Passenger Railway was electrified, and the remainder of the century saw a rapid increase in the transition to electric street car lines. The Baltimore and Ohio had long labored under a prohibition of steam locomotive operation within the City of Baltimore. Trains were pulled by horses through the city for many years, a circumstance that caused great concern for Abraham Lincoln's safety when his train passed through that bastion of Southern sympathizers on the way to his 1861 inauguration. Baltimore was the site of the first electrification of a main-line railroad, with the completion of four miles of electrified track that included a tunnel.

A press pass for the 20th Century Limited's first run.

The twentieth century brought better labor conditions and a decline in bitter railroad disputes like the 1894 Pullman Strike, which sent federal troops into the yards.

The first electrification plan for the Central was drawn up by William J Wilgus, vice-presdient and chief engineer. His basic idea was to use multiple levels for expansion rather than spreading out on the surface of Manhattan's high-priced terrain. Wilgus proposed the use of electric locomotives for suburban trains running in the two outside Park Avenue tunnels. South of 56th Street, the existing cut would be widened, and a loop of track would be laid under the old Grand Central Station and adjacent areas. Subterranean operations of this kind were feasible only with electric traction.

Wilgus's plan was approved by the Central, but the directors were slow in appropriating the millions of dollars necessary to carry it out. Procrastination vanished with the tunnel accident of 1902 and the subequent banning of steam locomotives in

A 2-6-6 Tank-type locomotive of the late nineteenth century, when American leadership in steam locomotion was acknowledged even by British railroad pioneers.

Some 11,000 of these 2-6-0
steam locomotives were built
in the United States.

Manhattan. Wilgus's plan was presented to the state as the Central's compliance with the new law.

Once the Central decided to electrify, the scope of the project went beyond Wilgus's proposal. The Central's 34-mile route to Croton and the 24 miles of track to White Plains were taken into the electrification plans, with service reaching White Plains in 1910 and Croton three years later.

The Central ordered 35 electric locomotives and 180 multiple-unit suburban electric cars. The latter were made possible by the American inventor Frank J Sprague, who invented the controller that made it possible to operate a string of these cars from one station in the lead car. Sprague had supervised the Richmond Union electrification and was Wilgus's major consultant. Electric operation started on a limited basis in 1906.

THE LOUNGE CAR . . .

In keeping with the other cars of The Mercury, the lounge car is of a distinctive and unusual type.

The semi-circular service bar is located midway of the car and is backed by a full length mirror.

THE PARLOR CAR . . .

Here again you find the large movable chairs, tables and reading lamps that give the informal and inviting atmosphere of home.

The warm colorings of tans, browns, rust and gold provide a restful background.

Hand baggage and coats are cared for in a space provided especially for the purpose.

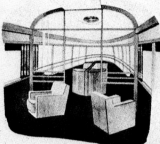

ONE END OF LOUNGE . . .

The lounge car is done in deep rich browns, rust, green and gold, and is furnished with luxurious movable chairs and built-in settees.

Tables are provided at convenient locations where passengers may be served with beverages or with food from the dining car.

The intimate grouping of the furniture gives the car the hospitable atmosphere found in a club.

PARLOR OBSERVATION CAR . . .

This car was built so that passengers can really "observe." Its streamlined, oval end with unusually broad windows and seats facing outward make it in every sense an observation car, where passengers may enjoy a full view of the passing scenery.

A special room at one end of the car is provided for checking hand baggage, coats and parcels.

Opposite, far left: *The major lines vied with one another in the opulence and comfort of their passenger cars.*

Right: *A pre-World War I ad focused on the female traveler.*

Left: *The Central ordered 35 electric locomotives when electrification began in the early twentieth century.*

Below: *This 4-6-2 Pacific-type locomotive (1903) would become a standard form of passenger power for decades.*

When she travels

Women traveling alone or with children prefer the famous limited trains of the New York Central Lines—because the standards of service on the restful *water level route* are such as they are accustomed to in their own homes.

Ladies' maids are in attendance on the *Twentieth Century Limited*, the *Lake Shore Limited* and the *Wolverine*—the three de luxe trains in the New York-Chicago service most favored by women travelers. On the *Century* facial massage and shampooing may be had in the barber shop in the club car.

The comfortable lounging room of the observation car is an added attraction on the *Century*, especially on the run along the famous Palisades and through the wonderful Highlands of the Hudson.*

★ *The westbound Century enters the Highlands at 3:50 p. m.; the eastbound at 8:10 a. m.*

Twenty through trains with Pullman sleeping cars are operated daily over the water level route of the New York Central Lines between the Grand Central Terminal, New York, and the two Chicago terminals—Central Station and La Salle Street Station

The Century
Westbound

Lv. New York .... 2:45 p. m.*
Lv. Boston ...... 12:30 p. m.*
Ar. Chicago ..... 9:45 a. m.*

Eastbound

Lv. Chicago ...... 12:40 p. m.*
Ar. Boston ...... 12:00 noon*
Ar. New York..... 9:40 a. m.*

*Standard Time
The water level route

NEW YORK CENTRAL LINES

NEW YORK CENTRAL

In 1903 Wilgus made a series of proposals that would completely change the character and appearance of midtown New York. He insisted that the old trainshed and station were not only inadequate, but architecturally out of step with surrounding structures. He proposed tearing them down and asked: 'Why not ... in their place, and in the yard on the north, create a double-level, under-surface terminal on which to superimpose office quarters and revenue-producing structures made possible by the intended use of electric motive power?'

A major component of the plan was depressing the tracks in the yard below street level, allowing restoration of the crosstown streets from 45th to 55th that had been so long interrupted by the yard. Since there was no longer any need to make allowances for the escape of smoke and steam, 'air rights' could be sold for

New Englanders resented Central control of their Boston & Albany Railroad so deeply that the words 'New York Central' were removed from all trains sent east of New York State.

A pioneer 0-8-0 built for the New York Central in 1916.

Main picture: *The streamlined 20th Century on an 80mph run along the Hudson River.*

Right: *The Century was drawn by a 4700-horsepower Hudson locomotive.*

Right: *The Century's menu catered to sophisticated and affluent travelers.*

TWENTIETH CENTURY LIMITED
ON THE NEW YORK CENTRAL.

DINNER

CONSOMME · BLUE POINTS

STUFFED MANGOES · PUREE OF TOMATOES
CALIFORNIA RIPE OLIVES · CELERY · QUEEN OLIVES · CHOW CHOW
SALTED ALMONDS · PIN-MONEY PICKLES

BAKED REDSNAPPER
CUCUMBERS

BROILED FRESH MUSHROOMS ON TOAST
SWEETBREAD BRAISED WITH SPINACH
RIBS OF PRIME BEEF · PEACH FRITTERS

MASHED POTATOES · ROAST CHICKEN WITH DRESSING
BAKED SWEET POTATOES
STRINGLESS BEANS IN CREAM · ASPARAGUS
CORN

ROMAN PUNCH

ROAST TEAL DUCK
LETTUCE AND EGG SALAD
WATERCRESS SALAD

CHARLOTTE RUSSE
ENGLISH PLUM PUDDING, HARD AND BRANDY SAUCE
NEAPOLITAN ICE CREAM · ASSORTED CAKES
CALIFORNIA NAVEL ORANGES · ORANGE MARMALADE
ROQUEFORT CHEESE · APPLES · GRAPES · BANANAS
PHILADELPHIA N.Y. CREAM CHEESE
MOHAWK VALLEY MILK AND CREAM
BENT'S CRACKERS
COFFEE DEMI-TASSE · TEA

No charge for coffee demi-tasse served in Buffet Smoking or Observation Car.
Please procure check from dining car conductor.

MEALS. ONE DOLLAR

"LITHIA POLARIS"—PURE SPRING WATER FREE.
The drinking water served on the New York Central Dining Cars is
from the celebrated "Polaris Springs" of the Boonville Mineral Spring Co.,
on the Rome, Watertown & Ogdensburg Division, in the foot-hills of the
Adirondack Mountains. It has been analysed by eminent chemists, and is
absolutely pure.

A SOUVENIR MENU.
A copy of this Menu card in an envelope ready for mailing will be
furnished free, on application, by the conductor in charge of this car.

construction of buildings over the tracks. Also included in Wilgus's proposal was the construction of a double-level, undersurface terminal. The lower level would include the loop for suburban trains. In the place of the old shed, an entirely new terminal and office building would be constructed.

Wilgus's plan bore a heavy price tag – $43 million – at a time when the federal budget was still counted in millions rather than billions. Nevertheless, the Central's board approved the plan, mainly because of the prospect of the huge revenues to be gained from air-rights structures.

New York City's Board of Estimate and Apportionment approved the plan in 1903, and the board's chief engineer was moved to comment: 'The plans impress me as providing perhaps the best railway terminal station in the world.' Work began that same year, and although there were many changes in the plans, and no small amount of controversy and acrimony over the design of the terminal building, the Grand Central Terminal that was completed in 1913 was much as Wilgus had envisioned the structure.

Once the basic plan was approved, the Central invited architects to submit design proposals. As might be expected, some of the most distinguished architectural firms of the day submitted proposals. Stanford White proposed a 700-foot office tower that would feature a 300-foot jet of steam issuing from the

Opposite, top: A few of the original 1-D-1 (now 2-D-2) electric locomotives are still in service on Conrail.
Opposite, below: The Class T electric locomotive had a top speed of 75mph and was designed for long-distance service. This one was built in 1926.
Below: A double-end type 2-4-4-T in suburban service, 1910.

top of the building. Illuminated by red lights at night, the steam would serve as a beacon to mariners. Other contenders included Daniel H Burnham, who had designed the Flatiron Building, New York's first skyscraper, and who had just received the commission to design Washington's Union Station. The contract for the Grand Central design went to a realtively unknown firm from St Paul, Minnesota – Reed and Stem. The design work was carried out by Charles Reed.

One of the major design problems revolved about what to do with Park Avenue. An abrupt end to this thoroughfare at either end of the terminal was not acceptable. Stanford White had proposed an arched passage for the avenue right through the terminal. The solution that was eventually adopted was Reed's proposal for an elevated 'circumferential driveaway' to take Park Avenue around the terminal. At this writing, the drive is still in place and in very active use. Reed's proposals for the lofty main concourse, and for wide, gently sloping ramps for moving people between the street and the two levels, were also adopted.

Although Reed and Stem had won the competition, they were induced to associate with the New York firm of Warren and Wetmore. The fact that Whitney Warren, senior member of the firm, was William K Vanderbilt's cousin and close friend, was no doubt an essential factor in this selection. Cousin or not, Warren was an extremely talented and imaginative architect. He had studied at the Ecole des Beaux-Arts in Paris, and had been briefly associated with Stanford White's firm of McKim, Mead, and White.

The inclusion of two brilliant artists on the same project might have been expected to cause conflict and controversy, and that is exactly what happened. Plans were changed and changed again. Reed's original plan for a 'court of honor' between 45th and 48th

Above: Eastward, Westward
*by Walter L Greene shows the
great Buffalo terminal.*

Left: *Another Greene
painting:* When Winter
Comes.

Opposite: *Greene's paintings
conveyed the power and pride
of the Central's halcyon days.*

Streets was abandoned and resurrected several times before its final discard. Also discarded was Reed's original plan for a high offie building above the terminal. Charles Reed died in 1911, and soon thereafter the Warren and Wetmore firm was awarded an exclusive contract for completing the work. Allen Stem, the surviving partner of the firm of Reed and Stem, sued over distribution of the fees. In the 1921 settlement, Warren and Wetmore paid him some $400,000.

The final version of Grand Central Terminal has been widely described as 'Beaux Arts Eclectic.' Built largely in Stony Creek (Connecticut) granite, the 42nd Street facade is set off by three 33-foot-wide and 60-foot-high arched windows flanked by Doric columns. A huge clock topped by a statuary group featuring figures from mythology – Mercury flanked by Hercules and Minerva – is situated above the center window. The entire design, particularly the heroic statue, was widely and roundly criticized. However, no one could deny that the design certainly gave credence to the direction-giver's assurance of 'You can't miss it.'

The interior earned a great deal more praise than did the grandiose exteriors. The lofty windows serve to give an airy feeling to the main concourse, which is 275 feet long, 120 feet wide and 125 feet high. The most familiar feature to the millions of travelers who walk through this concourse is the circular information booth in the center.

Travelers who look up will be rewarded by a view of the great astronomical mural painted on the ceiling. Based on a design by the French artist Paul Helleu, the mural depicts a Mediterranean winter sky, including some 2500 stars and paintings of zodiac figures in gold against a cerulean-blue tempera background. The 60 largest stars in the constellations are provided with electric lighting that is adjusted to indicate the correct magnitude. It was soon noted, however, that the zodiac was backward.

Grand Central Terminal was completed in 1913. In that same year, the New York Central and Hudson Railroad was reorganized. The various constituent roads such as the Hudson River Railroad and the Lake Shore and Michigan Southern were abolished as separate entities and completely absorbed into the parent organization, now called simply the New York Central Railroad.

The selling of air rights proved to be very successful. The last available building site was taken before the end of the 1920s, and the area over the tracks soon became one of the city's most expensive and prestigious commercial districts. Among the air-rights buildings is the Waldorf-Astoria Hotel, the only hotel in the world with its own underground railroad siding. The 34-story New York Central Building was constructed in 1929. Now called the Vanderbilt Building, it stands right at the Park Avenue centerline between 45th and 46th Streets. The 59-story Pan Am Building, completed in 1964, competely changed the Park Avenue view. It was placed to the north of the terminal, so you can still see Mercury with his arms outstretched over the clock. However, the north facade of the terminal is obscured. Banks of moving stairs take people directly from the concourse to the Pan Am Building.

The Grand Central complex is a city within a city. It has been said that you could spend your entire life beneath the surface in

Below: *Architects' rendering dated 1910.*
Opposite: *The main concourse.*

Following pages: *A Central train passing through East Rochester – and into history – in the late 1960s.*

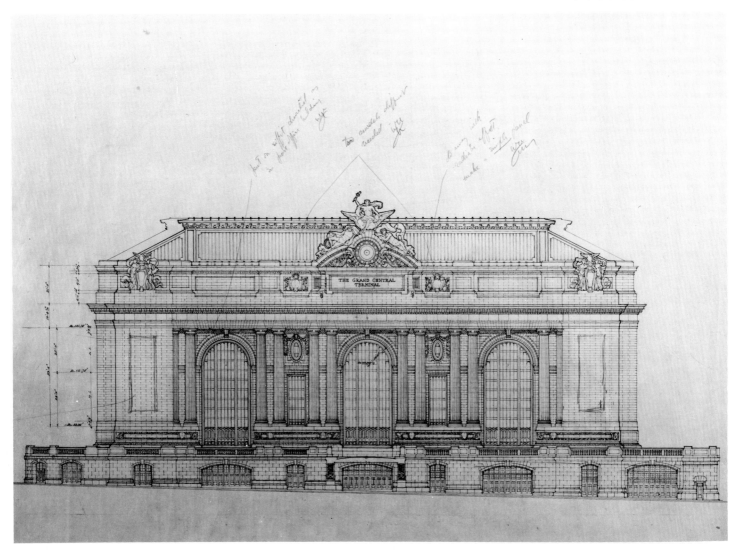

that maze of passageways without having to emerge for any product or service. There are stores that sell just about any merchandise one might need. More than 100 restaurants, one of the best bakeries in the city, a post office and even an emergency hospital are to be found in this complex.

A stroller on midtown Park Avenue today can see no evidence that beneath him is one of the largest in-city railroad yards in the world, with some 57 tracks and platforms. However, if you stand at the southeast corner of the intersection of Park Avenue and 46th Street — where the elevated roadway descends to the northbound lanes of Park Avenue — you can definitely feel the pavement shake and bounce in response to the traffic. This mobility is a reminder that a great man-made cavern is directly beneath you.

Although Grand Central is still one of the major railroad stations of the world, someone seeing it today for the first time in 20 or 30 years could not fail to notice obvious signs of decay that are in many ways a monument to the rapid decline suffered by the New York Central and railroads in general since the end of World War II.

CHAPTER SIX

DECLINE,
MERGER, AND
COLLAPSE

The post-World War II version of the Twentieth Century Limited was inaugurated in 1948 with a ceremony featuring the presence of Dwight D Eisenhower (not yet president) and the singer Beatrice Lillie. The champagne bottle Miss Lillie smashed against the observation car was filled not with champagne, but with waters from the Mohawk and Hudson Rivers and from the Great Lakes. The observation car no longer had an open platform. Like the rest of the train, it was streamlined, and featured an aerodynamically designed curved rear end.

This little ceremony around the newly modernized Twentieth Century Limited was supposed to herald a postwar era of prosperity for the New York Central. While the Century was bright and new, those who rode ordinary Central trains could see the unmistakable signs of trouble. The paint on the cars was peeling, windows were dirty and seat upholstery was likely to have unrepaired rips. The bouncing, lurching ride on shoddy roadbeds was a sure sign of 'deferred maintenance,' a euphemism for not spending on necesary repairs so that profit and loss statements would look a little better.

After the war, Americans hungered to get back into their automobiles, and the air lines surged into their war-postponed expansion. Both the air lines and the automobile makers were helped by the government – at taxpayers' expense. Federally funded programs sped construction of highways and airports, while tax-paying railroads continued to be hobbled by thousands of ICC regulations.

Of course, the Central was not alone its woes; all American railroads suffered to some degree from competition with automobiles and airplanes. However, the Central was paticularly vulnerable to competition from automobiles, buses and trucks. Its routes were short compared to those of such Western lines as the Union Pacific. Shippers generally found it more expedient and economical to use trucks rather than the railroad for short hauls. The Central was running nearly empty trains, both pas-

Below: *A summary of the postwar plight of the railroads.*

Right: *Eisenhower, Bea Lillie and Mayor O'Dwyer.*

The observation car Sandy Creek on the 20th Century, seen here in Chicago in 1965.

senger and freight, on some of its short feeder lines, but could not get ICC approval to discontinue the service.

While the decline of railroads was most dramatically obvious in the post-World War II era, their troubles had started even before the First World War. By 1916 more than 37,000 miles of railroad line were in receivership. The outbreak of war in Europe had resulted in a sharp increase in traffic for American railroads, as manufacturers, particularly those in the northeast, were flooded with orders from warring nations. The Central had to borrow money to buy new locomotives and rolling stock, but the ICC would not allow an increase in rates. Like the rest of American industry, the railroads had to go along with the 1916 law mandating an eight-hour day. While this law was a great victory for American workers, the railroads could not raise their rates to cover the added labor costs without ICC approval, which was not forthcoming.

When the United States entered the war in 1917, the financial condition of most American railroads, including the New York Central, was not particularly strong. The car shortages, broken track and other consequences of 'deferred maintenance' made it extremely difficult for the railroads to meet the increased demands of an America at war. Attempts of Eastern railroads to pool equipment failed becuase there was not enough equipment to pool.

During the war, the railroads were nationalized and placed under the direction of William G McAdoo, President Wilson's son-in-law. McAdoo invited his old friend Alfred H Smith — president of the New York Central — to be the regional director for Eastern lines.

When the lines were returned, they were in bad repair. In 1920 over a billion dollars was spent on railroad maintenance — a new record. Most railroads propsered along with the rest of the country in the postwar boom. The Central and the Pennylvania spent lavishly on electrification, while other lines waited to see if anything would develop with diesel locomotives. Thus the Central entered the Great Depression with a large debt. In 1932 its revenues were $293 million, but its funded debt was $670 million. This situation was reflected in Central stock, which de-

Main picture: *The originator of this powerful 2-6-6-2 articulated locomotive was Frenchman Anatole Mallet; 1300 of these engines were built in the United States.*

Right: *A Class Ala 2-8-4 Berkshire-type locomotive in heavy-freight service.*

This powerful 4-8-4 type of locomotive was first built for the Northern Pacific Railroad. Some 1000 engines of this type ran on American rails in the last great days of steam.

A gleaming 4-8-2 Mountain-type locomotive built for the Central by the American Locomotive Company (Alco).

clined from 130 in the spring of 1931 to less than 10 in the autumn of 1932. That year was the first in the long history of the Central that it did not pay a dividend.

Although the Central did not go bankrupt during the Great Depression, it became a very shabby operation. More than two-thirds of its passenger cars and more than half of its locomotives were over 20 years old by the close of the decade. However, there were no cutbacks for the Twentieth Century Limited, which continued to be the nation's premier train.

During World War II, the Central ran to capacity, as did most other lines. So many people rode the trains during the war years that the government tried to discourage travel with such tactics as posters bearing the message 'Is this trip necessary?' The Central was able to reduce much of its long-term debt, and its stock, which had been as low as 7 in 1942, was up to 35 by the end of the war.

Other railroads survived the postwar rush to automobiles and airplanes, and the Central might have too, had it not been the

Main picture: *Hudson locomotives like this 4-6-4 hauled the Century until they were replaced by diesels in the 1950s.*

Right: *A mid-1940s Niagara locomotive equipped with 'elephant ears' to disperse smoke.*

victim of stock raiders and poor management. The Central's demise could be said to have begun with the emergence of the strange financial empire of the Van Sweringen brothers.

Oris Paxton and James Mantis Van Sweringen were not the usual stuff of which big-business tycoons are made. The two bachelors, who lived together in a small house in Cleveland, sold real estate in and around that city. In the 1910s they developed a suburb called Shaker Heights. In those days, automobiles were not in every driveway, and the usual way to get to downtown Cleveland from Shaker Heights was on the street car. The Van Sweringens got the idea that if they could provide better transportation in the form of an electric railroad, the value of their Shaker Heights property would improve. Oris and James Paxton didn't know a whit about railroads, but they did know Alfred Smith, the President of the New York Central, who also happened to live in Cleveland.

In 1915 the Van Sweringens went to Smith for advice, and he gave them much more than that. The ICC had been pressuring the Central to divest itself of the Nickel Plate Road. Smith was not opposed to this: the Central needed cash and the sale of the road would be a good way to raise it. However, he had been unable to find a buyer. Smith saw his opportunity with the Van Sweringens, and before they knew what had happened, the two rather bland real estate brokers from Cleveland found themselves in the railroad business. Smith offered to sell them the Nickel Plate for $8.5 million, a bargain price. Of course, the brothers didn't have $8.5 million, but the House of Morgan took care of that, by organizing a securities company to sell stock to pay for the purchase.

Thus began a financial empire that seemed to have issued from

Left: *A 1940s ad based on a poll of wartime passengers.*   Below: *A postwar RS-1.*

the pages of *Alice in Wonderland* rather than the banking houses of Wall Street. The Van Sweringen enterprise grew into a Medusa-like tangle of holding companies manipulating the stock of some of the largest railroads in the country, including the Missouri Pacific, the Erie, and the Chesapeake and Ohio. Theoretically, the Van Sweringens were worth more than $3 billion, but their empire was a house of cards, existing mainly to provide a paper base for stock manipulation rather than to run railroads. As for the two brothers, they hardly knew what was happening. The old joke about the tycoons not knowing what they owned or how much money they had was no joke in this situation – it was just about the only reality.

The Van Sweringen empire fell apart in the Great Depression, but it was pasted together by loan on top of loan from the Morgan interests. The banks soon tired of this game, and in 1935 they foreclosed, putting the Van Sweringen properties on the auction block.

George Ball, who had made millions selling home canning jars, was a friend of the Van Sweringens, and had been on the board of the Nickel Plate, even though he knew or cared little about railroads. What he did care about was Eastern bankers – he hated them, and his primary reason for getting involved in the Van Sweringen mess was his personal sectional war, pitting Midwest against East. He formed a holding company called Midamerica, which bought Allegheny, the major Van Sweringen holding company. With this deal, the canning king had control of a railroad system with more miles of track than the whole of Great Britain.

Ball did not want to own this railroad empire, but he was determined to keep it out of the hands of those arrogant Easter-

Right: *Robert R Young, whose six-year campaign for control of the Central succeeded in 1954.*

Below: *The Central station at Briarcliff Manor, New York.*

ners. So when Robert Young, a brash young stock manipulator from Texas, expressed interest, Ball was ready to talk turkey. Young knew as little about railroading as any of the other players in this drama, nor had he ever been in an executive position. He had learned stock manipulation when he held a minor office job with General Motors, handling the affairs of some resident stock speculators.

Young eventually gained control of the Ball interests, despite opposition from Wall Street and even though he was unable to meet his payments to Ball, whom he sued on ground that Ball had manipulated stock prices, thus preventing Young from earning enough to meet the payments. The case had little merit, but Ball was close to 80 and getting tired; he was reduced to seeking advice from the hated Morgans in his fight with Young. Both he and the Morgans gave in and let Young have Allegheny and the C&O.

The next act in the play came in 1944, when a Federal Court ruled that the Pullman Company was a monopoly, and advised that it would have to sell either its manufacturing or its service division. The Pullman Company opted for the latter, and suggested that the various companies using Pullman cars buy the service division and operate it as a jointly owned subsidiary. The Central liked the idea, but the Pennsylvania did not, and blocked the deal. In stepped Young, offering to be the buyer. The New York Central did not want Young to have Pullman and eventually succeeded in stopping him. Young had dreams of starting the first real coast-to-coast passenger service, and ran his fight with the Central like a political campaign, projecting an image of himself as the reformer who was fighting entrenched interests for the good of the common man. He ran a famous ad showing a family group looking at a cigar-smoking pig in a freight car, with the legend: 'A hog can cross the country without changing trains – but YOU can't!' The Central had beat him, but Young knew he would have his day. He determined to raid the Central and have it for himself.

Above: *A Penn Central freight car in the classification yard at Selkirk, New York.*
Below: *The A H Smith Memorial Bridge at Castleton, New York, seen from the east.*
Opposite: *Alfred E Perlman, head of the Central when it merged with the Pennsylvania Railroad.*

No 3132 was one of a vanishing breed when this picture was taken (early 1950s).

The Boston and Albany retained its own name on Central rolling stock for generations.

Young's first attmept to gain control of the Central came in 1948. By the end of January, his Allegheny holding company had bought 250,000 shares, and Young demanded a seat on the Central board. The Central kept Young out with the help of the ICC. By this time, Young had become a media event and was widely regarded as a crusader. He continued his campaign, buying shares here and there, employing a strategy not unlike that of Cornelius Vanderbilt.

The fight for control of the Central reached a climax in 1954. The country had been in a recession since the previous year, and the Central reported a deficit of $5.2 million. Young pulled out the stops and started a campaign containing as much bally-hoo and hoopla as any presidential contest. He ran full-page newspaper ads blaming the Central management for the poor showing. He was on television talk shows. Supporters wore campaign buttons bearing such legends as 'Young at Heart.' Volunteers went door to door, soliciting the votes of stockholders. White won the fight by more than a million proxies, assuming control in mid-1954. There were no longer any Vanderbilts on the Commodore's railroad.

As soon as Young took over, the Central started to do better, an upturn that was due to the economic recovery rather than to Young's executive skills – and he knew it. The Central was a sick operation, in need of managerial miracles, and with that possibility in mind Young named Alfred Perlman of the Denver and Rio Grande Western as chief executive officer of the Central.

It would seem that Perlman knew how to run a railroad. He had saved the D&RG, and Young had every reason to hope that the young prodigy (graduated from MIT at age 20) could save the Central. Perlman charged into his work with a ruthlessness previously unknown on the Central, immediately cutting the work force by some 15,000. He virtually ignored passenger service, concentrating on modernizing freight operations. Commuter cars were allowed to disintegrate, and there was little the hapless commuters could do about it. Perlman did make one major change in passenger service: day coaches were added to the Twentieth Century Limited in 1957, forever tarnishing that famous train's glamourous image. In 1967 the Century was discontinued.

While Perlman was an efficient railroad manager, he was also a realist; he knew there was little hope for the Central without government help. The government had helped to build the New York Thruway and the St Lawrence Seaway, both of which were draining the Central's freight revenues; thus the government owed some help to the railroads, Perlman felt, and so testified at Congressional hearings. When federal help did not materialize, he turned to the only remaining option – merger.

Through the late 1950s and the early 1960s, Perlman approached a number of roads to talk merger. Of course, the Central was not the only line to seek salvation by this means: it seemed that merger fever had descended on the American railroad scene. However, few roads seemed interested in the Central. He was snubbed by the B&O, the C&O and several others. The Central's arch-rival, the Pennsylvania Railroad, had also been looking into mergers without much success. It slowly dawned on these two roads that about the only option left was the unthinkable. To many observers, a political union between the United States and the Soviet Union seemed a more likely possibility than a merger of the Central and the Pennsy.

Nevertheless, Young had several meetings with James Symes, chairman of the Pennsylvania. They continued their conversations through 1958, and appeared to be getting along with each other (Perlman was not involved in the talks at this point). All

Opposite, top: *An RS-11 switcher of the late 1950s, when diesel power had come into its own.*
Opposite, bottom: *A hood-unit diesel locomotive from the Central's last pre-merger days.*
Below: *An RS-32 built in 1961.*

An American Locomotive Company diesel passenger locomotive (PA-2) with a 16-cylinder, 4-stroke engine, built in 1959.

seemed to be going well when, on 25 January 1958, Young killed himself with a shotgun in the study of his Palm Beach mansion. Perlman continued the talks with Syme, although the two men did not particularly like each other, and the merger plans seemed to stall. Meanwhile, the Pennsylvania had diversified into interests ranging from oil pipeline companies to real estate and amusement parks.

The merger agreement was finally worked out in 1961. However, the necessary ICC approvals and the resolution of all the court cases instituted to stop it delayed the actual merger until 1968. The deal was also delayed by the ICC's insistence that the bankrupt New York, New Haven, and Hartford be included. Neither the Central nor the Pennsy wanted to take in the New Haven. This once-great road was now a shambles, the victim of stock raiders and the Connecticut Turnpike. It was saddled with an unprofitable but essential commuter service to New York City. Central and Pennsy executives knew they would have to include the New Haven if their merger was to be approved, and so they reluctantly agreed.

Perlman was not happy with the deal, knowing that it was more of an absorption of the Central by the Pennsy than a true merger. In 1963 Symes retired and was replaced by Stuart Saunders, who disliked Perlman even more than Symes did. The outlook for the newly formed Pennsylvania New York Central Transportation Company, better known as Penn Central, did not seem bright.

The Penn Central was in financial distress almost from the beginning. The organization of the company created a New York-Philadelphia dichotomy that made it even more difficult for the Central and Pennsy people to work together. Transportation operations were run mainly from New York by ex-Central executives, while the other interests, like real estate and amusement parks, were directed from Philadelphia offices.

Confusion was rampant. Freight trains were actually 'lost,' only to turn up hundreds of miles from their appointed destina-

tions. Of course, shippers would not tolerate this kind of thing, and many gave their business to trucks. It seems there were basic differences of operating philosophy between Central and Pennsy people that prevented a smooth combined operation.

The inevitable final conflict between Perlman and Saunders came in 1969. Perlman wanted $25 million to refurbish freight cars. Saunders said no, and Perlman retorted with a threat to resign if he didn't get the funds. Saunders accepted Perlman's resignation, and Perlman was not too sad to go, since it was now clear that the days of the Penn Central were numbered.

In the first quarter of 1970, losses in the transportation division of Penn Central exceeded $100 million. However, through fund transfers and various paper shufflings, the loss was made to appear minimal. The Penn Central started to look around for funds, and couldn't have picked a worse time: the country was in

Main picture: *The landmark water tower at Dewitt, New York, recalls railroading's early days.*
Opposite, top: *The 4083, painted jade green, passes through Utica in August 1962.*
Right: *The Penn Central was a new entity when this picture was taken in 1968.*

Above: *Penn Central suffered from polarization: railroad interests vs outside interests acquired by the 'Pennsy' before the merger.*

Opposite: *Amtrak was formed in 1971, the year after Penn Central lost over $100 million in its transportation division.*

Main picture: *A freight train in Wayneport in the late 1960s, when many dissatisfied shippers were turning to trucks.*

The legend 'Road to the Future' on this Central System train in Urbana, Illinois, had a hollow ring by 1966.

a double bind of recession and inflation. The stock market plunged. In a sense, the Penn Central gained time by the recession: the Nixon Adminstration feared that its failure at that time might cause a 1929-style panic. Penn Central executives used this as a lever to get government-guaranteed loans. The Penn Central's true situation was clearly shown when the economy had an upturn in spring 1970. The road lost $12 million.

The final outcome seemed assured when the same banks that the Penn Central was begging for loans started to sell their Penn Central stock. The railroad's executives had gone to Washington to seek help from the Department of Transportation. Secretary of Transportation John Volpe was sympathetic, and helped to work out a plan whereby the Department of Defense would guarantee loans for the Penn Central. After much debate in Congress, the plan was rejected. The Penn Central had nothing left to do but declare bankruptcy.

The bankrupt railroad continued to operate under a board of trustees. The Metroliner service between New York and Washington continued to be popular and fully booked. Over the next few years, the same government that had denied loan guarantees gave the Penn Central $150 million, and even

guaranteed a $100-million loan, knowing fully that American taxpayers would never see that money again. Nevertheless, the line continued to lose hundreds of millions although the economy was booming.

Amtrak came into existence on 1 May 1971. Under the provisions of the act that created it, railroads could give up their best passenger equipment to Amtrak in exchange for permission to discontinue their long-distance passenger service. The Penn Central certainly agreed. No one dared to say it out loud, but it seemed that the United States now had a national railroad, for without massive federal subsidies, Amtrak could not survive.

The Penn Central was almost abolished completely when, in 1973, the trustees said that unless financial aid were forthcoming, the railroad would be ordered to stop all operations by 1 October. The ultimatum stirred action in Congress, and the word nationalization was actually heard in serious tones. The Congressional action was the Rail Revitalization and Regulatory Reform Act, whose ultimate result was the Consolidated Rail Corporation, or ConRail. A precursor creature of the Act, the United States Railway Association, proceeded to cut some 12,000 miles of track from Penn Central's operation. In accord-

New York Central's 4000 in 1964, on its last run.

ance with the Act's provisions for bankrupt railroads to turn over their assets to ConRail, what was left went to that organization. By 1976 Penn Central was no more, as ConRail took over the Penn Central offices in Philadelphia.

Main picture: *No 4013 in 1965, four years after agreement of the Penn Central merger.*

Right: *Diesel power has no serious competitor on American rails; its takeover coincided with World War II.*

Previous pages: *Amtrak's impressive new equipment has enhanced its campaign to repopularize rail travel.*

Below: *Grand Central Terminal's heroic facade has seen vast changes in the fortunes of American railroading.*

Grand Central Terminal is still in existence, although there is constant talk of tearing it down to make way for another faceless glass-and-steel office building. You can still take a train to Albany or Chicago from Grand Central, and ride the 'water level route' along the banks of the Hudson and Mohawk Rivers and the Great Lakes shore. Amtrak trains are new, shiny and often on time, but even Amtrak officials know these trains are only shadows of what once thundered down these tracks. George Featherstonaugh might not be entirely happy with what he would see today, but he would still have the satisfaction of knowing that he had started one of the greatest chapters in American railroad history.

Amtrak's Turbotrain along the Hudson.

INDEX

Page numbers in italics refer to illustrations.

accidents 19, 25, 26, *52,* 52, *54,* 67, 70
advertising *15, 17,* 33, *64,* 66, *75, 98,* 105, *114*
Albany (NY) 9, 10, *18,* 25, 3
Albany and Schenectady Railroad 19, 23
Albany City Bank 28
Albany Regency group 9
Allegheny Railroad 99, 100
Amtrak *4,* 8, *112,* 115, *120-21, 123,* 123
Astor, John Jacob 10
Attica (NY) 18
Attica and Buffalo Railroad 18, 19, 22
Auburn and Buffalo Railroad 19
Auburn and Syracuse Railroad 18, 19; route 18

baggage handling 22
Baldwin, Matthias 16
  locomotives *16*
Ball, George 99, 100
Baltimore and Ohio Railroad 23, 33, 55, 68
Bangs, George S 60
Barnum, P T 45
Batavia (NY) *8;* 18, 19
Batavia and Rochester Railroad 19
Best Friend of Charleston 16
Boston and Albany Railroad 33, 64, *76, 102*
Boston and Worcester Railroad 33
brake(s), air 19
Buffalo (NY) 18, 30
Buffalo and Lockport Railroad 19, 23
Buffalo and Rochester Railroad 19, 23
Buffalo and State Line 30, 31, 33
Buffalo, Lockport, and Niagara Falls Railroad 23
Burnham, Daniel 81

C & O Railroad 100
Camden and Amboy Line 12, *13*
Canadian railroads 30, 33, 46, 64
car(s): electric 73; on luxury trains 66
Carnegie, Andrew 33
Chamberling, Churchill 12
Chicago (IL) 33, 45
Chicago, Burlington and Quincy Railroad 31
Chicago World's Fair 64
Cleveland, Cincinnati, Chicago and St Louis line 64
Congress 8, 60, 105, 115
ConRail 8, 118
Cooper, Peter 12
Corning, Erastus 16, 22-25, 30, 33, 40-41, 45; personal empire of 24-25, 28, 30-31
couplings 16

Daniels, George 64, *65,* 66
Denver and Rio Grande Western Railroad 105
derailment 60, 64
Depew, Chauncey 47, 48
Depew (NY) 19
Dewitt Clinton *11,* 16, 64
Dewitt (NY) *111*
Drew, Daniel 31, 36, 41, 45, 46

Duane, James 10
Dudley, Plimmon 64

Eisenhower, Dwight D *88,* 88
electrification *See* locomotives; railroads
Empire State Express 64
engines *24, 27, 45;* cable-powered 12; horse-powered 18, 68
Erie Canal 8-10, 16, 17, 18, 23, 33
Erie Railroad 19, 23, 31, 33, *34-5,* 42, 45, 54, 55, 57
Erie 'wars' 44
Exposition Flyer 64

Fargo, William 412
Fast Mail *59,* 60
Featherstonaugh, George 8-10, 12
Fish, Nicholas 10
Fisk, Jim 44
Flying Devil 60
freight services 16, 17, 25, 48, 52, 92, *100,* 105, *109,* 109, 111, *114*

gauge(s) 31
Gibbons, Thomas 36
Gold Rush (1849) 36
Gould, Jay 44, 45
Grand Central Depot (Terminal) *42,* 45, *49,* 57-8, 60, *61,* 67, *122,* 123; air rights over 84; remodeling 75, 81 and design *83, 84, 85,* 84-5
'Grand Central Station' 67
Grand Trunk Rilroad 64
Great Depression 92, 96, 99
Great Western Railroad 30
Greene, Walter (artist) 82

Hayes, Rutherford B 55
Helleu, Paul 84
Highlands of the Hudson 1
Hudson River 33, 36; bridge 40-41
Hudson River Railroad 33, *41,* 40-41, 42, 44, 45, 84; *See also* West Shore line

Interstate Commerce Commission 48, 88, 92, 98, 109

Jervis, John B 10
John Bull 12

Keep, Henry 42, 46

labor, costs 92. *See also* strikes
Lake Shore and Michigan Southern *47,* 47, 84
Lake Shore Railroad *29,* 33, 45
legislation 8, 23, 45, 54, 67, 73; federal 48, 115, 118. *See also* New York State legislature
Lillie, Beatrice *88,* 88
Lincoln, Abraham 68
Lockport and Niagara Falls Railroad 19
Lockwood, LeGrand 42, 46
locomotives *13, 30,* 30, *56, 58,* 60, 66, *71, 75, 76,* 81, *93, 95, 97, 110;* building 16, 64; diesel 92, *104, 107, 118;* electrified 67, 70, 73, *75, 80;* fumes from 67, *97;* scheduling 57. *See also* engines; steam engines; streamlining
luxury trains 64-7, *74, 79*

McAdoo, William 92
Madison Square Garden 45
Mallet, Anatole 93
A Message to Garcia 64
Metroliner 115
Michigan Central Railroad 30, 31, 45
Mohawk and Hudson Rail Road *6-7, 9;* 9-16, *17;* charter 10; opening 16; route 9
Mohawk Valley Railroad 19, 23, 24
Morgan, J P 48, 98, 99

New Haven Railroad 45
New York and Harlem Railroad 33, *37,* 39-40, 44, 45
New York Central Building 85
New York Central Railroad 8, 18, 52, *117, 118;* connection/expansion of routes 30, 31, 33, 40, 42, 45-7, 64, 66 (and decline 88); employees/labor policies 54-5, 57, 105; financing 23, 28 (*See also* stock); mail service 60; management, battles 105, and policies 81, 98-100 (*See also* Penn Central); mergers *22,* 25, 28, 31, 41, 44, 45, 84, with Pennsylvania 105, 109; opening 25; repair, maintenance/improvement 54, 66, 70, 88, 92; presidencies 24, 40, 42, 47, 92, 109; public relations 64, *67;* stations *40,* 45, *48-9* (*See also* Grand Central Terminal)
New York Central and Hudson River Railroads 45, 84
New York City 25, *32,* 33, 45, 67, 75, 81, 84; attitude toward inner-city railroads 57-8
New York, Chicago, and St Louis Railroad 47
New York, New Haven, and Hartford Railroad 60, 109
New York State legislature 9, 16, 18, 19, 23, 30, 58, 67; bribery of 40, 44-5
New York Stock Exchange 28
New York, West Shore and Chicago Railroad 47
Niagara Falls (NY) 25
Niagara River Bridge *20-1,* 25, 26, 28, 30
Nicaragua, passage through 38
Nickel Plate Road 98
Northern Pacific Railroad 95

O'Dwyer, Paul *88*
Olcutt, Thomas 40

Pan Am Building 85
Panic of 1837, 18
Panic of 1873, 54
passenger service 16, 52, 60, 105 and fare rates 17-18, 92. *See also* luxury trains; railroads; steamboats
Penn Central Railroad 109, 111, *111, 112,* 115
Penn Central Transportation Company, failure of 8
Pennsylvania Limited 66
Pennsylvania Railroad 8, 33, 47, 48, 55, 66, 100, 105, 109

Pennsylvania Station 45
Perlman, Alfred E *101,* 105, 109, 111
Pittsburgh and Lake Erie line 47
politics *28;* influence on railroads 9, 16, 19, 23
Port Byron (NY) rebellion 52-3
profit and loss 25, 88, 111, 115
Pruyn, John 23, 28, 41
Pullman, George 478
Pullman cars 66
Pullman Company 100
public opinion 9, 16, 19, 33, 52, 60, 64, 67. *See also* New York Central, public relations
The Putnam 30

Rail Revitalization and Regulation Reform Act 115
railroad bridges 40-41, *100. See also* Niagara River Bridge
railroads, coast-to-coast 47, 100; competition 66, 100, 105 (*See also* Erie 'wars'); co-operation 22-4, 33, 40; connections 40-41, 42; construction 12, 16, 17, 19 (and restrictions 16, 18); decline *88,* 109, 111, 115, 118, 123; electrification of 70, 73; employee policy 22 (*See also* New York Central); financing 8, 9, 18, 24, 98-9, 109, 115 (*See also* profit and loss; stock) and investigations of 28; horse-powered 12; mergers 8, 19, 22-3, 31, 33, 40, 41, 46-7; land leases 45, 52 (*See also* Grand Central Terminal, air rights); line lengths 18, 23; nationalization 48, 92, 115; passenger services *15,* 22, 33, 60, 88, 92, 109, in World War II 96 (*See also* luxury trains); rates 33, 47-8; repair/maintenance/improvement 24, 25, 64, 66; rights of way 17; rolling stock/equipment 25, 28 (*See also* cars); routes 19, 66; tunnels 58, 67; westward expansion 30, 33, 42, 45
railroad conventions 33, and 'peace conference' 48
railroad stations *8, 40, 82, 99, 109. See also* specific stations
Reading Railroad 48
Reed, Charles 81
Reed and Stem (architects) 81
Richmond, Dean 31, 41
Richmond Union Passenger Railway 67, 73
Roebling, John A 26
Roebling, Washington 26
Roberts, George 48
Rochester (NY) 18
Rochester and Syracuse Railroad 19, 23
Rochester, Lockport, and Niagara Falls Railroad 19
Rockefeller, John D 33
Rome (NY) 19
'runners' 33
Rutter, James 47

safety, employee 54, *55;* passenger 12.

Sage, Russell 33
St Nicholas Agreement 33
Saunders, Stuart 109, 111
Schenectady (NY) 16
Schenectady and Troy Railroad 18-19, 22, 23, 24
shipping 33, 36, 38, 40, 88
Smith, Alfred H 92, 98
South Carolina Railroad 16
South Pennsylvania Railroad 48
speed, 17, 25, 52, 60; records 64, *66*, 66; of steam engines 16
Sprague, Frank 73
Spuyten Duyvil and Port Morris Railroad 45
steam engines 8, 12, 16, 18, *56*, 67, *71, 72*
steamboats 36, 41; linked to rail service 22
Stevens, John 9
stock, holdings and value 10, 12, 16, *19*, 19, 23, 24, 28, 31, 38-9, 42, 45, 48, 92, 98, 105, 115; counterfeit 45; manipulation of 39-40, 42, 44-5, 46, 90, 98-9, 109
streamlining *62-3*, 66, 88
strikes 54-5, *57*, 57, *69*
switching equipment *48*
Symes, James 105
Syracuse (NY) 17
Syracuse and Utica Direct Railroad 17, 19, 23
Syracuse and Utica Straight Railroad 19

tender(s) 16
Thomson, Frank 48
timetable(s) *22*
Tom Thumb 12
Tonawanda Railroad Company 16, 18, 19
track, construction 45, 52-3, 64 (of lowered 57-8, 67, 75, 81, 85), double 17, 19; four-track system 57, 60; 'strap' rails as 12, 19; 'T-rails' 12; tunneling 70
trains *See* luxury trains
transportation 8; competition with railroads 88, 96, 105, *114*; rail combined with other forms 22, 33
trolleys 19, 39
Troy (NY) 24, 33
Tweed, William *28*, 39
Twentieth Century Limited *4*, 64, 66-7, *78, 79*, 88, *91*, 96, 105

Union Pacific Railroad 47
United States: and government regulation of railroads 8, 88, 100, 105, 118; government contracts to railroads 16 (mail service 60); government intervention in railroads 55; and government loans to railroads 115. *See also* Congress
United States Railway Association 118
Utica and Schenectady line *16*, 16, 17, 19, 23, 24

Van Buren, Martin 12, 24
Van Rensselear, Stephen 9
Van Sweringen, James and Oris 98-9
Vanderbilt, Cornelius 33, *36*, 36-42, 46, 60; and railroad empire *38*, 38-46
Vanderbilt, William 40, 44, *44*, 45, 46-7, 48, *52*, 52, 57, 60, 64, 66
Vibbard, Chauncey *24*, 25
Volpe, John 115

Wagner, Webster 47-8
Wagner Palace Car Company 66
Walker, Jimmy 66
Walker, William 38
Warren, Whitney 81
'watering' stock 45
West Point Foundry 13, 16
West Shore Line 47-8
Westinghouse, George 19
White, Stanford 81
Wilgus, William 70, 73, 75
Wilkinson, John 17
Wilson, Woodrow 92

Young, Robert R *99*, 100, 105, 109

ACKNOWLEDGMENTS

Picture credits

Albany Institute of History and Art, McKinney Library: 1, 6-7, 9, 17, 18 19, 20-21, 22, 22-3, 24 (above), 25, 29, 32, 37, 40, 54, 55, 65, 67, 74 (top left), 82 (both), 83, 102-03 (bottom), 122-3

Alco Historic Photos: 24 (below), 26-7, 38-9, 58-9, 62-3, 70-71, 74 (top right and bottom), 76-7, 80 (both), 81, 92-3, 94-5 (both), 96-7 (both), 98 (below), 104 (both), 105, 106-07

Amtrak: 2-3, 113, 120-21, 124-5

Bison Picture Library: 90-91

Al Gorney: 86-7, 108-09 (both), 110-11 (all), 112, 114-15 (both), 116-17, 118-19 (both)

Kalmbach Publishing Co Photo Collection: 4-5, 10-11, 44, 53, 59, 88-9, 99 (both), 100 (top), 101

A E Klein: 16

Library of Congress: 8, 57, 68-9

New York Central System Historical Society, Inc, Purinton Collection: 12-13, 13, 30-31, 34-5, 36, 45, 46-7, 48, 50-51, 56 (both), 64, 72-3, 75 (right), 76-7 (below), 78 (above), 78-9, 85, 88 (below), 93 (top), 98 (top), 100 (bottom), 102-03 (top)

New York Historical Society, New York City: 41, 42-3, 49, 52, 60, 61

New York Public Library Picture Collection: 42 (above)

Bill Yenne: 14-15

Acknowledgments

The publisher would like to thank the following people who have helped in the preparation of this book: Ron Callow, who designed it; Robin L Sommer, who edited it; Mary R Raho, who did the picture research; and Cynthia Klein, who prepared the index.